JOSEPH LUZZI

My Two Italies

Joseph Luzzi, the first American-born child in his Italian family, holds a doctorate from Yale University and is a professor of Italian at Bard College. He is the author of *In a Dark Wood: What Dante Taught Me About Grief, Healing, and the Mysteries of Love*; *Romantic Europe and the Ghost of Italy*, which won the Aldo and Jeanne Scaglione Prize for Italian Studies from the Modern Language Association; and *A Cinema of Poetry: Aesthetics of the Italian Art Film*. An active critic, his essays and reviews have appeared in *The New York Times*, the *Los Angeles Times*, *Bookforum*, and *The Times Literary Supplement*. He is the author of the audio courses *In Michelangelo's Shadow: The Mystery of Modern Italy*; *The Blessed Lens: A History of Italian Cinema*; and *The Art of Reading*. His honors include an essay award from the Dante Society of America, a teaching prize from Yale, and a fellowship from the National Humanities Center. Luzzi lectures widely on Italy, literature, art, and film. Visit him online at www.JosephLuzzi.com, and follow him on Twitter at @LuzziJoseph.

ALSO BY JOSEPH LUZZI

In a Dark Wood: What Dante Taught Me About
Grief, Healing, and the Mysteries of Love

A Cinema of Poetry: Aesthetics of the Italian Art Film

Romantic Europe and the Ghost of Italy

MY TWO ITALIES

My Two Italies

JOSEPH LUZZI

Farrar, Straus and Giroux

New York

Farrar, Straus and Giroux
18 West 18th Street, New York 10011

Copyright © 2014 by Joseph Luzzi
Printed in the United States of America
Published in 2014 by Farrar, Straus and Giroux
First paperback edition, 2015

Owing to limitations of space, illustration credits can be found on page 207.

The Library of Congress has cataloged the hardcover edition as follows:
Luzzi, Joseph.
    My two Italies / Joseph Luzzi.
        pages   cm
    ISBN 978-0-374-29869-2 (hardback) — ISBN 978-0-374-70889-4 (ebook)
1. Luzzi, Joseph.   2. Luzzi, Joseph—Family.   3. Italy—Civilization.
4. Regionalism—Italy, Southern.   5. Regionalism—Italy, Northern.
6. Italian Americans—Ethnic identity.   7. Italian Americans—History.
8. Italianists—Italy—Biography.   9. Italy—Biography.   I. Title.

PC1064.L89 A3 2014
945.092092—dc23
[B]

2013039910

Paperback ISBN: 978-0-374-53539-1

Designed by Jonathan D. Lippincott

Farrar, Straus and Giroux books may be purchased for educational, business,
or promotional use. For information on bulk purchases, please contact the
Macmillan Corporate and Premium Sales Department at 1-800-221-7945,
extension 5442, or write to specialmarkets@macmillan.com.

www.fsgbooks.com
www.twitter.com/fsgbooks • www.facebook.com/fsgbooks

1   3   5   7   9   10   8   6   4   2

To Helena Baillie
incipit vita nova

Si vulissi sappiri i secreti e ra casa, dumanna i criaturri.

If you want to know the secrets of a family, ask the children.

—Calabrian proverb

Contents

Author's Note

This is a work of nonfiction; some names and identifying details have been changed to preserve anonymity. I drew on my journals, notes, interviews, and research—as well as my own memory—in reconstructing the events and personalities of this book, all of which come from real life. In creating this mix of history and narrative, both private and public, I have tried to honor the words of Italy's greatest novelist:

> We ourselves, with great diligence if nothing else, have examined and collated all the printed [accounts] and several unpublished ones, and most of the few official documents that have survived; and we have attempted, not to give the material the final form that it deserves, but at least to do something with it which has never been done before.

Without presuming to put words in Alessandro Manzoni's mouth, I think he means that however much a writer would like to solve the riddles of the past, he soon learns that the best he can hope for is to bring them truthfully and vividly to life—and leave any final decisions to the reader.

MY TWO ITALIES

after arriving. Maybe he saw my father whaling away on our poor goat, as was his habit, and realized he would be much better off with a real American family.

I took the rabbit in my arms. Circumstances had kept me from becoming an "animal person," but this guy, with his white fur and gentle eyes—a present from my favorite relative to boot—was different, just like Cumara Amandina, who was much more delicate than the bruiser Calabrian matrons who poured into our home on Sundays. I would cherish him, I swore to myself. I'd make sure that the creature enjoyed a different fate from Sam's. My mother and father smiled, Amandina gushed, and the bunny went back in his box.

That afternoon I imagined that the rabbit was resting while I played outside. In truth, he was about to face an ordeal that would have shocked even battle-scarred Sam. Apparently my mother and father weren't just admiring the rabbit's dreamy eyes; they were sizing up his haunches. I don't know what it took—my mother's usual two brisk whacks with a stick to the back of the skull or my father's preferred twist of the neck in his thick fingers—but by five p.m. my pet had become an entrée. I came into the kitchen to find him splayed out, his glycerine blue eyes lifeless and coated in oil, over a bed of roasted potatoes.

It took my mom an hour to calm me as she explained that she and my father hadn't tricked me. They had planned it all along and just assumed that I knew what was coming. She spoke with a smile. That was the worst of it: to her, destroying my pet was no different from weeding the garden.

I followed my mother to the kitchen table, slunk back into my abandoned seat, and, tears spilling onto my napkin, ate my pet rabbit.

•

When I went to sleep that night with a belly full of my god-mother's gift, I knew I had done something not necessarily wrong, but certainly strange: eating a pet bunny may have been acceptable in Acri, the Calabrian hill town where my family had lived before emigrating, but not in the suburban Rhode Island town where I grew up. I had to admit, the rabbit was delicious. But what if my friends found out? It wasn't just the slaughter that troubled me. It was the feeling that everything I was learning in school, seeing on television, and picking up from my friends was pulling me away from my family's world.

Around this time I was named to the Little League all-star team, a group of local boys who represented our town in a nationwide baseball tournament. After our third straight win, I came home bursting with joy: my cousin had pitched a no-hitter to advance us deep into the state play-offs. My eyes adjusted to the change in light as I entered my father's lair: the refurbished basement where he held court, seated at the head of the dinner table in near darkness to reduce the electricity bill.

"Papà, abbiamo vinto, abbiamo vinto!" ("We won, we won!") I exclaimed.

He fixed me with a shark's stare and spoke in Calabrian.

"I heard you made a fool out of yourself. And the whole town was watching."

I buried my face in my glove and ran from the room. It was not enough that I had been chosen for the team, nor that we had won. I batted .556 and fielded a flawless third base during that play-off run. But for my father all that mat-

tered was that one fateful at bat, when I waved at a pitch
nearly over my head, my hands squeezing the bat so hard that
they creased the grip. A home run in front of the town's
faithful would have brought me the approval that was missing in our split-level on Batterson Avenue. He was right: I
had strode into the path of the stitched leather ball, swung
from the heels, and—like all those who daydream in front of
fastballs—struck out.

I didn't realize this at the time, but my father was swing-
ing at wild pitches of his own—and gripping the bat just as
tightly as I was—as he struggled to hang on to his dimin-
ished Calabrian world.

On November 21, 1956, eleven years before I was born,
Pasquale Luzzi and his four children cleared customs at JFK
and joined his wife, Yolanda, in the United States. They were
emigrating from the poor region of Calabria in southern Italy.

My maternal grandfather, Carmine Crocco, had worked
in the United States from 1909 to 1923 as an itinerant gravedigger, mostly in New Jersey and Pennsylvania, before moving back to his Italian village. He had won citizenship because
of his U.S. military service in World War I, so my mother
earned the right to bring her family to the United States,
where—thanks to my father's lifetime of factory work—we
joined the middle class.

By the time I feasted on my Easter rabbit, we owned our
own home, a squat three-bedroom that somehow slept eight.
In true Italian American style, we lived mostly downstairs,
a cavern coated with cooking grease—and the seat of my

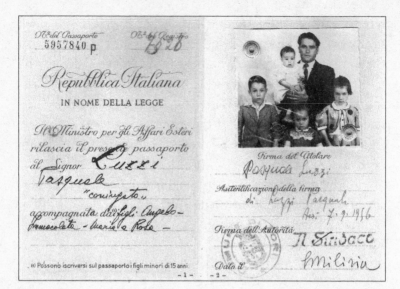

ABOVE: My father, Pasquale Luzzi, and family on his Italian passport (1956); LEFT: Naturalization papers of my maternal grandfather, Carmine Crocco (1919)

father's royal authority—while the upstairs furniture was kept protected from the human stain. Eventually I would attend an expensive private university (thanks to scholarships and financial aid) and wind up on a career path smoother than any child of Calabria could ever have hoped for. But first I had to escape the Italian south.

My parents described their region as a land with a blistering sun and an arid terrain, a ferocious 'Ndrangheta (the local Mafia), and an untranslatable worldview called *la miseria*, "the misery"—a pervasive belief born of poverty that things will go worse than you expect them to and that fate is not your friend. For my parents, *la miseria* meant stillborn babies, barefoot children, and no meat on the Sunday table. In their world, only the leather-tough and the single-minded (the *teste dure*, "hard heads")—blunt, tanklike men like my father and his four brothers—endured. Even today, when Calabrian immigrants speak of the future, they will often add the subjunctive disclaimer *"Si Dio vo'"* ("Should God will it"). The Calabrian God was one to fear, not to love, and the region he lorded over was no place for Grand Tourists seeking intimate encounters with Botticelli in the Uffizi. It was the quarry for men like the robust Norman Douglas and his *Old Calabria* (1915), a pioneering work in extreme travel writing:

> This corner of Magna Graecia is a severely parsimonious manifestation of nature. Rocks and waters! But these rocks and waters are actualities; the stuff whereof man is made. A landscape so luminous, so resolutely scornful of accessories, hints at brave and simple forms of expression; it brings us to the ground,

where we belong; it medicines to the disease of introspection and stimulates a capacity which we are in
danger of unlearning amid our morbid hyperborean
gloom—the capacity for honest contempt: contempt
of that scarecrow of a theory which would have us
neglect what is earthly, tangible.

This raw genealogy at once repelled and seduced me. I longed
to cure the disease of introspection—maybe Calabria would
make a man of me. So in the 1990s, while many of my friends
pursued lucrative careers on the new dot.com frontier, I
entered graduate school to study Italian literature: a gut decision in a life marked, then and since, by hedged bets. I hadn't
pursued the subject as an undergraduate; a vague attraction
to Dante's poetry was my only link to the field. And let's just
say my college transcript didn't inspire visions of an endowed
chair at a leafy New England university. When I asked one
of my professors for a letter of recommendation, he told me
I was a likable-enough kid, but really . . .

But even in those first fitful steps toward Italy, I felt
pulled by something more instinctual than academic clout
or a career calling. I wanted access to my family's history.
Yes, they had abandoned Italy for good, but a part of them
remained fixed in that blasted Calabrian landscape. Their
broken English, canned tomatoes and slaughtered pigs, homemade wine and cured meats—it all reeked of the Old Country. Especially the tripe. Some days I would come home
from school and burst into the house for an afternoon snack,
hoping for a buttered slab of my mom's freshly baked bread,
only to have my hunger stifled by the odor wafting up from a
downstairs pot. These were the days my mother boiled cow

stomach, the blanched organ that revealed just how different—
less refined, less American—we were from our neighbors,
with their vacuumed Pontiac Bonnevilles and pine-scented
air fresheners.

A career in the language and culture of my family would
immerse me in the mystery of their lost Italian world, which
sometimes felt like a birthright, more often a pipe dream.
Around 1304, Dante compared the nonexistent Italian language—at the time, Italy comprised various city-states and
their local dialects—to a scent that filled the air but whose
source could never be found. Italian culture was like that to
me. I sensed it all around—in the mildewed winepress and
hanging prosciutto shanks of our cellar, in the oily redness of
my mother's sauces and the leathery texture of her cured goat
cheese—but it was somehow remote from the "real" Italy,
with its Renaissance palaces, handmade leather goods, and
covered jewelry stalls on the Ponte Vecchio. My Ph.D. in Italian would be the passport to a cultural homeland that class,
history, and society had all conspired to deny me and my
family.

When I finally made it to Italy for the first time, as a college student in 1987, it was Florence and not Calabria that
beckoned. I yearned for the Italy of Dante and Michelangelo,
not the one of sharp cheese and salted anchovies. As soon as
I arrived, I felt the weight of the past in the crooked cobblestone streets and the sidewalks that barely held off the Vespas
straddled by women in chestnut lipstick and leather miniskirts.
Each day, I left my apartment near the bombastic arch of
Piazza della Libertà to walk down Via Cavour, the nineteenth-
century boulevard that connects the city's modern and medieval neighborhoods. My route to school skirted the market

of San Lorenzo, where stalls of fruit, bread, meat, clothing, and wine have been lining up like dominoes since the late 1800s. From there it was a short stroll east to the Duomo, begun in 1298 by Arnolfo da Cambio and completed by Filippo Brunelleschi in 1436. From this cobblestone womb of the city I would head west along the Corso and into the Piazza della Repubblica, the original site of the city, where the Romans—according to legend, Julius Caesar himself— established a military camp in the first century B.C. Once I had my espresso from the ornate Caffè Gilli, founded in 1733, I circled back east, south of the Duomo and into Santa Croce, the site of the basilica that houses the remains of the nation's founding fathers. There I would stand before the statue of Dante, nineteen feet high and keeping angry vigil over the stones of Santa Croce.

As seduced as I was by Florence, I still longed to under-stand the Italy of my parents. So on a cold and rainy November day of my first semester abroad, I boarded the train for Calabria. I felt like I was in Europe until we reached Naples. Then the journey slogged from one local stop to the next on antiquated lines and obsolete regional trains packed with southern Italian families laden with salami. When I finally arrived hours later in Cosenza, my parents' home province, I felt that I had lurched a century backward into a struggling nation, far from the smiling angels of Fra Angelico and the muscular women of Michelangelo. My blood is 100 percent Calabrian; I looked a lot like the young men milling about the station and piazzas. But the good people of Cosenza re-garded me as if I had alighted from a spaceship. Like twins shipped off to different homes at birth, our bodies declared a common biology, but our bearing, gestures, and clothes suggested otherwise. This was my first journey south, but I would discover the Italy of my parents only much later.

✳

"Sleep . . . is what Sicilians want, and they will always hate anyone who tries to wake them."

In 2003, as my Intercity train from Florence pulled into Napoli Centrale, I recalled these words from *The Leopard*, Lampedusa's great novel about the fall of the Italian aristocracy on the eve of national unification in 1861. We southern Italians, remarks Prince Salina, alias the Leopard, wish for nothing more than a "voluptuous immobility," free from the demands of history and innocent of the crimes committed in the name of progress.

Naples, the seat of the Bourbon dynasty that ruled the Leopard's Sicily, had been the capital of southern Italy since the Middle Ages. But after unification the city underwent a long decline. Millions of its children immigrated to Australia and the Americas, northern factories exploited its natural resources, and the organized crime movement—the Camorra—consolidated its local tyranny. In the early 1990s, however, Naples had emerged as a major European cultural center, especially in avant-garde and politically engaged film. Led by the dynamic mayor Antonio Bassolino from 1993 to 2000, the new Naples supposedly stood at the vanguard of a southern Italian renaissance. Teaching that summer in Florence, I had decided to travel south to witness the revival firsthand.

At least that's what I told people. In truth, I had come to see the capital city of my parents' homeland—the Mezzogiorno,

"Land of the Midday Sun," the nickname given to the Italian south because of its geographical location and, more figuratively, its relentless heat. For two decades I had been spending nearly all my time in Italy in Florence. I had even stopped visiting Calabria because I was tired of the suspicious looks that the locals gave me, of having to wash myself each morning in my uncle Giorgio's detached bathroom with its trickle of icy water. I was now a professor of Italian and a published scholar in that high culture that had been so remote from my childhood world of boiled tripe and aunts swathed in black. My parents' Italy was no longer my Italy, I told myself. But still, I owed it to them to see the heart of their southern Italian *patria*.

"See Naples and then die," the expression goes, and as my train made its way toward the Bay of Naples, I couldn't imagine an urban space more favored by nature. The hills along the shore spread into the city proper. The arches and columns that punctuate the metropolis recall the city's ancient Roman settlers, one of the few peoples from the Italian peninsula to rule Naples. The gentle symmetries and proportions of Italy's other cities pale in comparison with this awesome port of entry.

"Here you'll find the best and the worst," the Neapolitan lawyer seated beside me said. *"Siamo in un'altra Italia."*

Another Italy, indeed. I arrived to find pickpockets swarming the train doors, on the lookout for the markings of foreign prey: white sneakers and university logos, grinning American midwesterners in pressed chinos. In the sulfurous July air, the chaos of trams, taxis, kiosks, and buses made crossing the Piazza Garibaldi a sweaty ordeal. All the while I held my hand over my wallet.

My hotel room was accessible only by a dingy elevator in a courtyard that doubled as a loading zone. Though I'd been promised a room with amenities, construction delays would force me to use the communal bathroom in the hall. The receptionist deflected my protests by pointing to a caving plaster roof above him and lamenting, *"Nella camera con bagno, è ancora peggio."* I accepted his word that my original room was in worse shape than the mutilated reception area, picked up my keys, and headed in for a nap. To my amazement, the terrace of my room looked out onto the Bay of Naples and the looming Castel dell'Ovo fortress along the shore. For forty dollars a night, I had a room with a glorious view—but no toilet.

I spent the next few days sleepwalking. Each morning at around four a.m. a troop of Spaniards in town for a wedding dragged Naples's disco culture into the adjacent room and danced and sang until dawn. I complained to the receptionist, but he could only throw up his arms and provide a Neapolitan brand of reassurance: *"Eh, le regole purtroppo s'infrangono"* ("Well, the rules unfortunately get broken"). Neapolitans, I learned, often speak in the impersonal voice, symbolic of the powerlessness they feel in the face of fate.

But the sights. Whether the endless corridors of Renaissance painting in the Capodimonte Palace, the mummies and Greco-Roman statuary of the Archaeological Museum, or the delicately sculpted *Veiled Christ* and preserved human anatomical experiments ("the skeletons") in the baroque Sansevero Chapel, Naples offers cultural treasures that few cities can rival. A ghostly quality permeates these marvels. Since the city lies off the Rome-Florence-Venice tourist path, I often found myself alone in a room filled with priceless art. In the

Sansevero, I was one of only three to admire Sammartino's *Veiled Christ*; the security guards, ticket vendors, and other museum employees outnumbered us by a wide margin. The quiet disturbed me. Foreign rulers, especially the Spaniards, had hoarded the treasures of Naples in their palaces and temples for centuries. No Neapolitan ruler, Italian or foreign, had ever intended his trove for the people. One could say as much about most rulers and most collections, but in Naples, whose small middle class and teeming millions will probably never set foot in a Sansevero Chapel, there isn't even the pretense of art being for the masses.

Nearby Pompeii left me cold. I had already taken the trip in my mind a hundred times. I had imagined temples of Venus at sunset and ancient lovers wrapped in each other's arms, their passion eternally fixed in lava. I found instead droves of backpacking Germans, loud American student groups, and even louder Neapolitan tour guides, as well as a cafeteria specializing in french fries and fluorescent ices. Amid the dust and jostling of Pompeii's queues, I became nostalgic for the large, lonely rooms in the Capodimonte and the Museo Archeologico, however undemocratic.

After my visit to Pompeii I wandered around the center of Naples at dusk in search of a snack and film for my camera. The human density, which one has to see and smell to believe, choked the city's thoroughfares. Children rode past three to a seat on Vespas, and the tiny white Fiats appeared to be stacked one upon the other on the slender sidewalks. I found my film and a *sfogliatella*, the city's heavenly filo-dough ricotta pastry, then sat for a moment in the Piazza Dante. Into my ears wafted sentimental Italian folk music that, in my fatigue, brought me back to the plaintive accordions and fidgety tambourines of a Calabrian wedding. An attractive dark girl with teased eyelashes smoked on the bench beside me. Like many other women in town, she wore a touch too much makeup, colors too bold and poorly matched to boot. Around me swelled the *passeggiata*, the Italian ritual in which an entire town or city takes to the streets for an after-dinner stroll. In Naples, though, the casual conversation and gelato consumption of the north changes to boys with slicked hair swaggering past chaperoned young ladies, and old women in jewels led along by trim signori in black jackets. I had seen and heard it all before, in old family photographs, in the *Godfather* films, in that stack of cracked 45s my mother and father brought with them from Calabria. My mother would clean house to this music of her childhood, her body so enthralled by songs of festival days and forbidden love that the vacuum cleaner danced in her arms.

Here is my first homeland, I thought, *my Italian America!*

It all came back: the smells of my mother's kitchen, the icy stare of my father and its hint of possible violence, the stocky uncles in short sleeves and their callused hands, the shapeless aunts, the bazaar of my Calabrian childhood turned up at full volume in the Piazza Dante. My parents and their fellow immigrants would translate the world of downtown Naples into the discos, pizzerias, and social clubs of such places as Providence, Brooklyn, Buenos Aires, Sydney, and Toronto, but the seed of these diasporas, the point of origin to which no southern Italian son or daughter could ever return after having left it, was heartbreaking, impossible Naples. *"Napoli,"* cries a character in Pasolini's film *The Decameron*, "only those who lose you can love you!"

The night I discovered the urban soul of Italian America,

a toothless woman who had pitched camp in one of the city's traffic circles accosted me. I had noticed her the day I arrived and was astonished by the care she put into tidying up her asphalt enclave, a bunker of old clothes, ripped boxes, and discarded metal. My stay in Naples seemed to revolve around her: I passed by her junk-strewn roundabout each time I left the hotel or returned to my room from a meal or sightseeing. Walking by her after leaving the Piazza Dante, I looked back—just like Orpheus, when I wasn't supposed to—and caught her eye. A shock pulsed through me. Half in a trance, I took a moment to realize that she had sprung up from her filthy mound and was heading toward me, swearing at full pitch in a dialect that I thankfully could not understand. She was laughing, so I knew right away that she was not a good witch. I easily outdistanced her, but I can still picture her craggy, toothless smile. *Ti acchiappo, figlio mio. I'll get you, my boy,* her dead eyes say, *just come back to Naples, and I'll get you.*

That night, the Spaniards continued their revelry. I was sleep deprived and desperate to return to staid, graceful Florence. The witch would never catch me, for I'd been running from Naples my whole life. Though I was close to my Calabrian relatives as a boy, as I progressed through junior high and high school, I had little contact with the thirty-odd first cousins with whom I shared a last name. Consciously or not, the sports I played, the schools I attended, and the career I chose marked a distance between Calabria and me that was as lengthy as the Appenine spine separating Naples and Florence. *Staid, graceful Florence.* A city of the Renaissance, of Dante and Michelangelo, of unsalted bread and black cabbage soup. This was the Italy I had chosen, though I had inherited one of a very different shape, smell, and taste. Perhaps I deceived myself in thinking that I could ever outrun my southern Italian heritage. Maybe, in the end, all that separated me from the Mezzogiorno was a few advanced degrees and the desire to tell my story to strangers.

The next day, I arrived at the train station for the return trip to Florence, but officials casually informed me that a national rail strike, the dreaded *sciopero*, had taken effect. *I'm leaving the city,* I thought, *no matter what.* By then, seven o'clock in the evening, the bus services and travel agencies had closed. Frantic, I found a car rental agency run by a man named Carmine. He was locking up for the day; after hearing my story, he put down his keys. Within a half hour he had provided me with a sturdy Fiat, directions to Florence, brochures of his favorite hotel in Capri, and a compact disc with Neapolitan folk music. I must return to Naples, he insisted. I told him I was not sure that I would. He nodded his head in understanding.

Here you find the best and the worst, he said, echoing the words that the lawyer had told me upon my entrance to the city. *"È un'altra Italia."*

By nightfall, the highway had funneled me out of that other Italy and onto the long road north.

In 1818 the English poet Percy Bysshe Shelley wrote:

There are *two* Italies—one composed of the green earth and transparent sea, and the mighty ruins of ancient

time, and aërial mountains, and the warm and radiant
atmosphere which is interfused through all things.
The other consists of the Italians of the present day,
their works and ways. The one is the most sublime
and lovely contemplation that can be conceived by the
imagination of man; the other is the most degraded,
disgusting, and odious.

Shelley was scandalized by the contrast between Italy's fa-
bled history—which had inspired him to leave England and
spend the last years of his life as an Italian exile—and its
everyday miseries and corruptions. Echoes of Shelley's "two
Italies" thesis abound, including the recent book *Good Italy,
Bad Italy* by Bill Emmott, a former editor of *The Economist*
who distinguishes between *la Mala Italia* ("selfish, closed, un-
meritocratic, often criminal") and *la Buona Italia* ("open,
community-minded, and progressive").

I carried my own two Italies inside: the southern Italian
immigrant world of my childhood and the northern Italian cultural realm I devoted my adult life to. In the classic
story about the founding of Italy, Virgil's *Aeneid*, the hero
Aeneas greets the ghost of his father, Anchises, in the Under-
world. His father stretches out his hands and cries: "You've
come at last? Has the love your father hoped for / mastered the
hardship of the journey?" That word *hardship* recalls for me
the prodigious labor that immigration would exact from my
father, whose sacrifices resulted in no epic poem and who
left no empire in his wake.

One night, around the time I entered graduate school to
study Italian, he awoke and rose from bed to use the bathroom. He was once fiercely strong, shorter than most but built

like the proverbial brick shithouse. Now, years after a massive stroke, his left arm hung limp against his body; his barely functioning left leg, withered to a chicken shank, left a gap between his skin and his underwear; and his testicles drooped in the sagging cotton as he dragged himself down the hallway. His factory had recently honored him with a plaque that now hung on his bedroom wall. Twenty-five years of service. That quarter century had meant waking up at three thirty a.m. to start work at five (his shift began at seven, but he arrived early to log overtime). He spent the next ten hours powering a lathe in the din—and then, weather permitting, a few hours more landscaping at a second job.

After relieving himself, my father limped back to bed beneath the plaque. This new world, which had given me so much, had taken everything from him. He had acted of his own free will. But the journey north from the Mezzogiorno had broken him in body, in spirit, and in soul.

Or so I thought. When I became a parent myself, I understood that his story was not only about self-denial. It may not have seemed like much to me, but to him that plaque symbolized a lifetime of honest labor that had brought tangible rewards: money in the bank, a house and car of his own, schools and jobs for his kids, even a few acres of investment property. In Calabria, these things were unimaginable for my father, one of eight children raised on dirt floors.

My daughter, Isabel, was born in 2007, four years after my return from Naples and a full half century after my parents abandoned Norman Douglas's gloomy corner of Magna Graecia. Commentators used to agonize over whether to hyphenate *Italian American* or leave the words untethered. Should the two ethnic identities be left separate to signal their cultural uniqueness, or be brought together in a symbolic union? My mother and father, for their part, didn't think of themselves as Italian or American, let alone the fusion of these terms. They were *calabresi*. For them, the "Italian-American" hyphen, like America itself, was a bloodless abstraction. I also had little time for the hyphen. I was Italian *and* American— a little of each, yet not fully either. And definitely not their seamless hybrid. It is left to my daughter's generation to inhabit the hyphen.

With each passing year, with each Calabrian relative that dies, with each Calabrian turn of phrase that is forgotten, the land of my parents fades from memory. At night I read to Isabel in hopes that she will learn to love stories and appreciate language, in the way that books helped me make sense of a country that was foreign to my own family. Stories will be all that binds her to Calabria. She will never be chased by a Witch of Naples, never come to dinner to find a slaughtered pet served over a bed of potatoes. I used to think of my two Italies as a burden, an ethnic cross I had to bear as I struggled to make my mark in the new world that my parents had brought me to. I was right: it was a struggle, one that I might have been happier without. But it was also the gift that brought me inside the disappearing world of my parents and millions of other Italian exiles—a distant land that my daughter may only ever know in translation.

PART I

THE SOUTHERN QUESTION

1

Carnal Violence

On July 25, 1943, the Fascist government of Benito Mussolini collapsed after a series of disastrous military campaigns in Europe and Africa. Less than two months later, Prime Minister Pietro Badoglio, who had been one of Mussolini's leading officials, announced that Italy was pulling out of its alliance with Germany and joining the Allied forces. With this staggering about-face, six hundred thousand Italian troops found themselves in a state of deadly limbo. Needless to say, Hitler was not pleased: the fury he had been directing at the Jewish people would soon find another target in his former allies. The Nazis promptly seized the Italian soldiers under their command and declared them "military internees," thus denying them the rights granted to prisoners of war. My father, Pasquale Luzzi, was one of these men.

The Germans stripped him of his weapons and shipped him from the Greek front to Bavaria. He nearly died of starvation in transit. At one point he went foraging for a raw potato and was beaten with the butt of a gun by a German soldier. A small number of military internees refused to work out of principle and were denied food; the vast majority, my father

included, did what they were told under pain of death. He
had no idea what the principle of a free and united Italy was.
For him, Italy was Calabria, and Calabria was a test of endurance, not an idea.

Another time, a German soldier ordered him to dig a
ditch. Exhausted, he refused. The soldier unloaded a fury of
obscenities on my father and then dragged him away to fin-
ish him off. An officer witnessed the scuffle and commanded
the soldier to stop. My father was released amid more shout-
ing and curses. Over the years, I have thought many times,
What was my father thinking? Why didn't he just dig? I never
dared to ask him.

In 1944 Pasquale arrived in the outskirts of Munich at
the farm of a municipal official—a man he called *il mare-
sciallo*, "the marshal"—who lived with his beautiful niece
Hilda. Her husband had been killed in the war. She noticed
my father right away; he studiously avoided her. If he was
caught with her, it could mean his death. Yet if he continued
to defy her advances, this too could prove fatal, for she could
report him as insubordinate. Eventually she made him an offer he could not refuse. I have often imagined the thrill of love
with his blond, voluptuous captor. A tremor of her discon-
tent and he was finished. But the relationship flourished. The
weeks stretched into months, the months into years. Before
they knew it, the war was over, and they were still together.

After the surrender of Germany, in 1945, Hilda and my
father were married. He believed that this would keep the
Germans from killing him. Though she was pregnant with
his child, he was restless. The war had been a parallel uni-
verse. As he continued to work on her farm, that first thrill
of their clandestine meetings tapered into domestic routine,

and my father knew that he could never be at home in Germany. Calabria was his *paese*. He wanted to go back.

Hilda sensed that he was eager to leave, so she was extra vigilant in monitoring his whereabouts. He tried to get her to relax her guard, and one day he insisted that she attend a faraway festival—she'd have a ball, he was sure of it. While she was away, he fled the farm by stealing a boy's bicycle. Eventually he made it past the German border, through Austria, and into Italy, where he began the long train ride south to Calabria. My father always spoke wistfully about his time in the Bavarian countryside. Though he had been beaten within an inch of his life at least once—for stealing that potato— and narrowly escaped execution another time, his years in Germany seemed to be among the happiest in his life. He

War Cross of Merit awarded to my father for his internment in Nazi Germany (1963)

vowed to my mother that he would return to Bavaria with her one day, and that he would show her his Germany. He never did make it—nor did he ever find out whether Hilda gave birth to a son or a daughter.

In 1963, eighteen years after my father escaped his captors and his pregnant wife, the Italian Army awarded him the War Cross of Merit for *"internamento in Germania."*

※

A half century after my father's flight from Germany, I spoke at an Italian American society before an audience of about twelve—several of whom were my family members. I discussed the hidden connections between Italian culture with a capital *C* (Dante, the Renaissance, Michelangelo's *David*) and Italian American culture (Rocky, Tony Soprano, spaghetti and meatballs). After the presentation, a member of the audience compared the small crowd with the one that had been attracted by another Italian American, Nicole "Snooki" Polizzi from the television program *Jersey Shore*. I was told that there had been "lines going out the door" at her recent book signing at the nearby Barnes and Noble. Ms. Polizzi once earned $32,000 for an appearance at Rutgers—$2,000 more than the Noble laureate Toni Morrison received for a talk there, and $32,000 more than I earned that evening. *Jersey Shore* also generates its share of social capital: in 2012, the University of Chicago hosted an academic conference devoted to "Jersey Shore Studies," which included the panel "The Construction of Guido Identity" and the paper "Foucault's Going to the Jersey Shore, Bitch!"

Aesthetically speaking, *Jersey Shore* stands at ground zero of the Italian American look. For all their cruelty, the mobsters in Coppola's *Godfather* films cut a fine figure, especially the Vito Corleone played by Robert De Niro. Things took a turn for the worse in the suburban chic of Tony and Carmela Soprano, who favored such prêt-à-porter items as leisure shirts and matching pantsuits. If the Corleones were always prepared for a wedding or a christening, the Sopranos looked primed for the bowling alley or an evening out in Jersey's Little Italy.

But nothing could presage the fashion atom bomb of their kindred on the New Jersey coast. In season four, Snooki and friends traveled to the city of Dante and Michelangelo, where, according to *The New York Times*, they staged "a cultural collision between working-class Italian-Americans who favor fake tans and gold chains and call themselves guidos, and Florentines, who are among the most elegant and snooty of all Italians." Tracksuits, push-up bras, tanning spray, animal-print suitcases—all the brash signifiers of Italian America were on display. Dante described his quest for the elusive Italian language as the hunt for a fragrant panther that knew its way around the woods; Snooki in her trademark leopard print advertised her ethnic identity with decidedly less mystery.

Not long ago, Snooki's public appearance in a shirt with "Brunette Mafia" emblazoned on it would have rallied the troops. In November 2001, I watched the critic Camille Paglia stride onto the podium of Logan Hall at the University of Pennsylvania to speak on the topic "Tony Soprano, the Media, and Popular Culture." The HBO program *The Sopranos* was inaccurate, she claimed, not because it portrayed Italian men as murderous mafiosi, but because it showed them as vulnerable and introspective, nothing like the manly types she

LEFT: Robert De Niro as the young Vito Corleone in *The Godfather: Part II* (1974); BELOW: Tony and Carmela Soprano, all dressed up

recalled from her childhood. Her Italian men didn't slump as Tony did on some psychiatrist's couch; they rolled out covered in grease from underneath cars. The firebrand Paglia is nothing if not original, and her elegy to the biceps of Italian America riled the earnest Ivy League auditorium. But she produced some howlers. She railed against a putative New York "haute bourgeoisie" that refused to live up to its ideals of multiculturalism. If this group understood *The Sopranos*, she said, it would own up to its "heavy guilt trip" about race, realize that its idea of society was "white," and see that "the whole thing about *The Sopranos* is a cryptic version of dealing with race issues in this country." She marched ahead:

> The fact that [*The Sopranos*] shows that Italian Americans are literally the last group that people are free to libel means that all Italian Americans have to start banding together and realizing that's why this is so pernicious—because the educational system in America at the public-school level and the college level has moved away from the Western tradition.

Despite her overheated syntax, Paglia failed to diagnose the real issue about the show. It's not because of race that the Mafia remains our great Italian American foundation myth, our *Iliad* and *Odyssey*, a *Paradise Lost* but never regained. History, Marx wrote, happens first as tragedy then repeats itself as farce. Initially we had the Shakespearean drama of Coppola's star-crossed Corleone family, then the suburban sprawl of the Sopranos. Before, mythic Sicily, historic Greenwich Village, and a family man played by De Niro/Brando; after, Snooki giving birth on her own reality show.

About a year after Paglia's speech, Mayor Michael Bloomberg of New York invited two stars from *The Sopranos* to march in the Columbus Day Parade. Claiming that the show promoted negative stereotypes about Italian Americans, the organizers of the parade protested. Bloomberg held firm, skipped the parade, and spent the afternoon of Columbus Day eating Italian food on Arthur Avenue in the Bronx with his two friends Lorraine Bracco (Tony Soprano's psychiatrist, Dr. Jennifer Melfi) and Dominic Chianese (Tony's surrogate dad and predecessor as the family *capo*, Uncle Junior). Is *The Sopranos* good for us, many of us wondered, good for Italian America?

Although this debacle has faded from memory, the controversy it symbolizes endures. Whether we like it or not, and whether inside or outside Little Italy, the Mob remains a myth as irrepressible as the honor of Vito Corleone. No wonder most Americans separate Italy, the Land of Dante, from Italian America, the Turf of Tony Soprano and Snooki. We Italian Americans suffer from a form of cultural schizophrenia, half of our soul nourished by centuries of European arts and letters, the other half contaminated by Luca Brasis and Jackie Apriles. Many organizations have decried this cultural duality and argued for more representative images for Americans of Italian descent. After all, Italian Americans have produced the Yankee Clipper, two Supreme Court justices, a woman vice presidential candidate, four mayors of New York City, and three governors of New York. Yet for all that Italian Americans accomplish, we can't seem to wash mobster blood off our hands. As Tony Soprano might say, *You know, we're not really like them, those* 'mericani. He might add, *We Italian Americans, we're not really like them either, those* italiani—*you know, the real deal you get over in Italy.* The outcry against unsavory media representation of Italian Americans reflects the unease that many in this ethnic group feel toward the Old Country, Italy itself. In fact, the hullabaloo about *The Sopranos* had less to do with the preeminence of the Mob as Italian America's most enduring stereotype than with the historical melancholy of something called the Southern Question.

When Italian Americans claim cultural ancestry in the land of Dante, Galileo, Michelangelo, and the like, they're engaging in a public act of wish fulfillment. These titans hailed from northern Italy, which has historically been the seat of the nation's political power, material wealth, and cultural innovation. This isn't to say that the south lacks an illustrious history of its own. No serious student of Italian culture fails to absorb the value of such movements as the medieval Sicilian School of poetry and the artistic ferment of baroque Naples, or of such southern intellectuals as Giordano Bruno, Giambattista Vico, Francesco De Sanctis, and Benedetto Croce. The fact remains, however, that the Italian north has traditionally viewed the south as a massive *altro*, "other." As a political quandary, the Mezzogiorno is associated with the Southern Question, the ominous phrase Italians have used since time immemorial to describe the difference between the so-called first world, above Rome, and what many call the "African" territories to Rome's south.

The great majority of Italian Americans, Tony Soprano and associates included, hail from the Mezzogiorno. Although Italians have been immigrating to America from as far back as the 1700s, the notion of an Italian American came into existence only after the period of mass emigration from southern Italy to the United States in the late 1800s. Before then, an intrepid few made the journey not to escape poverty, but to make their mark in an exciting young country. In 1778 a former Florentine tailor named Carlo Bellini became the first chairman of modern languages at an American college, William and Mary, where he taught Italian, French, German, and Spanish. Bellini also served in Virginia's foreign office and counted Thomas Jefferson as one of his friends. Lorenzo da Ponte, the Venetian adventurer, memoirist, playwright, and librettist for Mozart, taught for many years at Columbia, where today a chair of Italian studies is named in his honor. Who would label these Enlightenment literati "Italian Americans"? In order to qualify for that designation, you have to carry inside at least a bit of *la miseria*. Unlike these scholars, Italian Americans generally don't consider *l'America* to be a mere step on the career ladder. The inflated rhetoric of immigration (Old Country, New World, American Dream, melting pot) suggests how high the stakes are for those who, like the Italians who arrived during the waves of mass exodus, abandoned their *patria* out of necessity rather than choice. Many southern Italian immigrants, my family included, carry within an invisible scar that goes by the name "The Italy I Never Knew."

Against the backdrop of the Southern Question, the great American myth of the Mob begins to make sense. *The Godfather* and *The Sopranos* offer an American morality play of upward mobility through the acquisition of power, money, and prestige. Where else might Italian Americans turn for their master narrative—to *Rocky*? To powerful but less known literary works such as Pietro di Donato's *Christ in Concrete*, a story of working-class struggle in Depression-era New York, or the cascade of autobiographical writing by authors

ranging from John Fante and Jerry Mangione to Helen
Barolini and Gay Talese? None of the above manages the
epic scope of *The Godfather,* and none exhibits the tragicomic
melancholy of *The Sopranos.* Nor have they inspired the public to ponder the mysteries of Italian American identity on a
broad scale. I don't think that the great Italian American book
or film will ever be created. Such a story would require a
powerful organizing myth. We Italian Americans, on the
other hand, commemorate our past only to remind ourselves
how far we have traveled from it. Our pride in our ancestors
grows with the distance we set between them and ourselves.

※

Family legend has it that my mother was so overwhelmed
when she first met my father, in 1946, the year he fled Germany, that she sputtered chestnut meat on his military uniform. She was young, but her family owned land, and my
dad decided on the spot that she was the one, though he had
recently broken off an engagement to another woman in their
Calabrian village—and though he had just abandoned his
pregnant wife in Bavaria. In truth, my mother wasn't eating
chestnuts then, and my father wasn't wearing a uniform. But
the image persists: she was probably afraid of him, as we, his
six children, would be. After all, my father was a man who
had shared all those stolen, secret nights with his delicious
blond captor, the threat of death hanging over each embrace.
My mom was a virgin, kindhearted, never more than a few
paces away from her father's or brothers' gaze. She didn't stand
a chance.

My mother's name, Yolanda, never sounded Italian to

me. Nor did she look typically Calabrian, with her dramatic full features, her tight curls, and darker coloring than most of her fellow villagers. But when you watch her clean the house, her ethnicity is never in question. She handles children, dispatches animals, plants tomatoes, and hangs laundry with a care I've seen only in southern Italian women. Her youth was no different: she went from one sunrise chore to the next in her village—feeding the livestock, watering the garden, and gathering the vegetables—and to the evening tasks of preparing the meal, cleaning the stalls, and retrieving the laundry. She dreamed of being a schoolteacher but only reached the fifth grade. Still, she had it much better than almost every other Calabrian girl she knew. The tracts dividing her house from the mountains belonged to her father, Carmine Crocco, who purchased the land with the money he had made burying thousands of Americans for fourteen years before returning to Italy for good at age thirty-two—around the age my father was when he left Italy to immigrate to America. Every few weeks or so in the United States my grandfather sent money to his wife, Rosaria, in Calabria, which she used to purchase real estate: Calabrian gold. Eventually Carmine could no longer tolerate the rotted heads and limbs of improperly interred corpses, and his nerves began the steady decline that sent him into an early old age. He had tried to find alternate work in America, in a textile mill, but the fumes overwhelmed what was left of his resistance. It was time for him to return to Calabria.

The dollars that Carmine Crocco had wrung out of America's cemeteries made him prosperous back in his village, where he spent his days overseeing his properties. All the locals wanted to work for him because he was the only

Italian identity card of my mother, Yolanda Luzzi. Her profession is listed as *casalinga*, "housewife" (1953)

landowner who paid them fairly. But my grandfather's nerves, the same family malady that later rendered my mother an insomniac, continued to unravel him. A thin man with a broom of a mustache, he had lived away from home too long to enjoy his prosperity, and it showed in his eyes.

His twenty-two-year-old son Angelo died from an illness he had picked up while serving in the Italian Navy during World War II. A doctor in Naples had misdiagnosed Angelo with malaria and given him the wrong treatment. By the time the family found out the true nature of his sickness, it was time to bury him.

The death of his youngest boy, Francesco, at seventeen months from pneumonia pushed my grandfather over the

TOP LEFT: Carmine Crocco of Acri, Province of Cosenza; TOP RIGHT: my maternal uncle, Angelo Crocco, member of the *Bersaglieri* (Marksmen), a special corps of the Italian Navy in World War II; ABOVE: Carmine Crocco and a friend in the Calabrian countryside

edge. His sorrow became so unbearable that his family decided to take in Giorgio, the illegitimate child of a local peasant woman, to look after the sheep and keep my grandfather company. Meanwhile, everyone still wanted to work for Zio Carmine ("Uncle" Carmine, as he was called with affection and respect) because he paid more than anyone else. Despite the sadness of its paterfamilias, the family flourished. My mother even slept in her own room.

My father's village was "down mountain," about an hour's walk from my mother's more desirable "up-mountain" village. As trying as Germany had been, at least in the end my father had been his own boss there, with a new family, a household to run, and the exhilaration of having survived what so many of his friends and enemies had not. In Calabria it was back to the manure, the stingy land, the virginal women, and a tyrannical father. He needed another place to escape to. His sister Rosaria mentioned to my father that Zio Carmine's young daughter, Yolanda, would soon be available. Pasquale decided to pay a visit.

One evening while she was roasting chestnuts, my mother spotted a well-dressed man entering her family's property. He said hello to her and proceeded to speak with her father and mother. Nothing much else happened. Pasquale liked what he saw and began to visit often. A few days later he stopped by on the way to a wedding with some candied almonds. This was her first gift from him. The visits became less formal and my father's feelings more manifest. He and my uncle Giorgio, Zio Carmine's adopted son, often serenaded their beloveds, Pasquale's Yolanda on one side of the village and Giorgio's Filomena on the other. (It was hard to believe that the Filomena I came to know, a squat seventy-year-old matron with whiskers, missing teeth, and a purple boil on her lip, could have inspired such rapture.) Then suddenly, inexplicably it seemed to Pasquale, Yolanda went to sleep early on the evening of one of his visits, when she knew he had come to see her, knew that he had made the long journey on foot for this purpose and no other. In Pasquale's mind there was no more need for the charade: Zio Carmine had agreed to the marriage and given his blessing to both Pasquale and his father. But my mother had heard of another suitor in a nearby village, and she was so young— it was all happening so quickly. *"Eru 'na guagliuna,"* she said. "I was just a kid."

"He was a good, kind man," she said of Pasquale's rival. "I wanted to see him." She knew my father's story: he had left his pregnant wife behind in Germany; he had fled his captors turned kin; he had a child in the land of the fair-skinned enemy. Pasquale had hidden all this from everyone but Yolanda.

The day after she snubbed my father, local elections were held in the village. My grandfather Carmine, who held this to be so sacred a rite that he would lose his U.S. citizenship over it, wanted to participate with his wife. They were reluctant, however, to leave their daughter unattended. But Yolanda's younger brother Giovanni was at home with her, so they decided to go. Later that morning, Pasquale and his brother Giancarlo showed up at my mother's house. Giancarlo accosted Giovanni in the yard while he was tending sheep and tied him up. Meanwhile, Pasquale burst into the house, brandishing a revolver.

"I'm going to rape you," he said to my mother. "Stay still, or I'll shoot you!"

"You can shoot me," she answered, "but you will not rape me."

Pasquale reached for her, and she fended him off with a pair of scissors. Outside the house, Giovanni began to shout, and soon a host of villagers showed up on the property. After some time, Pasquale emerged from the house with his shirt ripped and his revolver in hand. My mother swears that nothing happened, that she sat on a crate the entire time they were inside and repeated to him, "Shoot me, but I'm not coming near you." Afterward Pasquale told Zia Rosaria, Yolanda's mother, that he still wanted to marry her daughter, even after assaulting her. Fine, she answered, but she also wanted to know exactly what he did. My father swore that he didn't rape Yolanda—he was just trying to scare her and, more important, make her shame public.

The act was a ritual of sorts in the region; it went by the term *acchiappare*—"to grab" or take someone by force to create the impression (actual or fictitious) of a sexual conquest, so that the *acchiappata*, "seized," party would be dishonored and hence suitable for marriage only with the person who had supposedly laid his dirty hands on her. But it carried its risks, legal and affective. My father was charged with two crimes by the local judiciary: *violenza carnale*, "carnal violence," or rape, and *omicidio mancato*, "attempted homicide." In Calabria, there was no issue of dropping charges. The state acted as prosecutor and pursued the case irrespective of the possibly harmed party's wishes. The judge on my father's case came up with a brilliant, operatic solution: unless Yolanda agreed to marry Pasquale, he would be sent to prison. Pasquale's father, Federico, wept at the verdict: his family faced ruin.

Meanwhile, the other suitor, whose affections had instigated my mother's refusal of Pasquale in the first place, remained steadfast in his intentions. He swore that even if Yolanda had been violated—even if she was pregnant—he would still marry her. As far as I know, my mother has only ever been with one man, her husband of half a century, Pasquale. But this other villager who gently pursued her in the Calabrian hills still manages to elicit pangs from her. He died in the 1980s from a brain tumor after living in Argentina for decades. My mother met him once at the home of a mutual relative in New Jersey, and she said that he gave her a strange, imploring look.

Yolanda agreed to marry Pasquale. She couldn't bear the thought of him being sent to prison on her account. *"Eppure gli volevo bene,"* she said: "And still, I loved him." They were officially wed on August 17, 1946, so the criminal charges against him were dropped. My mother was fourteen years and eight months old.

After the wedding my father returned to his family and she to hers so that they could prepare for their life together. But after a few months with his family, Pasquale and his father reached the point of no return. He moved out. He asked Zia Rosaria—my grandmother—if he could stay with her, and she agreed (a quarter century later, after Zio Carmine died and Rosaria joined our family in America, my father accused her of being nosy and sent her back to Calabria in a rage). During this intermission Pasquale and Yolanda lived under the same roof as husband and wife in name, but not in fact. It was not until they moved into their own home, on March 17, 1947, that they consummated their marriage vows. She swore that, again, he hadn't touched her during those months they were living together at her parents after the official marriage. They had only one fight in that period, when he brought home a dog. Never one for pets, she kicked the yapping beast.

For the next fifty years my parents fought like a cat and a dog trapped in one of Zio Carmine's coffins. They slept in separate beds for as long as I remember, and they performed an endless series of small deceptions behind each other's back (my father, through his Scrooge-like grip on the family finances; my mother, with her secret doling out of favors to her children). Yet all their actions aimed at keeping the family intact, and their love for each other was as unshakable as the regulations my father issued to everyone under his roof. They finally left Calabria when my father could no longer bear the poverty. I don't know what he expected America to provide other than more money, and I think he was too old at the time—not in years, but in experience—to harbor illusions about anything as naive as an American Dream. But he was ready to work.

My mother, for her part, was prepared to join him and do whatever she could for her family. It was she, in fact, who was able to get her husband and then four children citizenship because of Zio Carmine's ties to America. But first she had to spend a year of residency alone in the United States. She seldom talks about this interlude. I imagine it was her version of my father's wartime Germany, a rare space apart from the family that defined her life.

My mother didn't follow fashion and current events. She still spoke Calabrian, never learned proper English, and expected her children to respect the customs of the ancestral home. No funny business for the girls before their wedding night, and no housework for the boys, whose bread she buttered from childhood to college. But she was no anachronism. If the girls were supposed to hold on to their honor till marriage, that didn't mean they always needed a male family member to look after them. Let them be free, she believed, and they'll know better. And we all did stay out of trouble, by and large, but only partly because of our good judgment. Mostly it was because we were terrified of what our father would do if we fell out of line. He punished us physically only on rare occasions, but he administered his curses as though they were the lashes of a belt, and the welts of shame stung just as much as their physical counterparts. No matter what he did, his dignity remained intact; hitting his children was beneath him. Besides, with a tongue as sharp as his, there was no need to waste such energy.

But Pasquale was having a worse time of it in the United States than Yolanda. He *did* seem anachronistic, though in a charming way—he would never set foot in a mall or wear the sweatpants and football jerseys of the *'mericani*. My father wanted this vast superpower, the ancient Rome of the modern age, to conform to his worldview. Great men often do, and sometimes they have the power, money, or good luck to bring the world in line with their vision. But he could not speak the language of his host country and did not give a dried fig for this new culture. So he expected his children, and especially his wife, to live as if they were in the Old Country—not the Italy of Verdi and Vivaldi, but the one of Zio Carmine and Zia Rosaria, who remained behind in Calabria and are now buried there.

Meanwhile, my mother went with the flow. When my father banned my sister Rose from home because she had the nerve to move out on her own (she was single and twenty-seven), my mother worked to broker a peace accord. When I insisted on going to a private college and brought home the fees for my boutique liberal arts education—in my father's defense, my academic performance warranted no subsidy—my mother pleaded with him to help pay the bill. When Rose could no longer bear to clip my father's yellow toenails and exercise his limp arm after his stroke, my mother reasoned with him that these tasks weren't suitable for a young, single woman—which is exactly what they were in my father's view. In his Calabria, unmarried daughters tended to their sick fathers with nunlike devotion. Pasquale Luzzi, a fierce, ethnic Lear roaring across the plain of old age, cursed the shortcomings of his children in proportion to the love he bore them. His life began and ended with his family, but everything that *l'America* taught his children seemed to weaken their connection to him. Poor Lear had only a fool to calm him, whereas my father was lucky enough to have my mother. Slowly, with each year that passed between them, with each domestic disaster averted either because of my father's will or my mother's diplomacy, the center held.

But their new country exhausted them. My father would fall asleep at the dinner table after a sixteen-hour workday, the basement rife with his snores and his breath reeking of stewed meat, cigarette smoke, and red wine. My mother was doomed to sleepless nights in every corner of the house, from the foldout sofa in the living room to the bedrooms vacated by siblings on their way to marriage and new lives elsewhere. There was a lot of passion between my parents while I was growing up, not the cooing kind, but the stuff it takes to hold together a family of six kids.

Love and hate, yes; intimacy and tenderness, no. At least not until their time together reached its winter. After my father's massive stroke at age fifty-nine, he depended on my mother for everything. She fed, bathed, and changed him. He was her baby now, and the situation infuriated him. But the physical proximity also had a mellowing effect. My father understood that in America in the 1980s and 1990s there weren't too many women who would spend their days tending to an invalid. He never said as much, but he began to show appreciation by hounding her less about her household duties and agreeing more when she asked him to help their children.

In his last, mightiest act of heroism—one that surpassed even his survival of enforced labor in wartime Germany and a Calabrian judge's nearly sentencing him to prison—Pasquale Luzzi defeated biology itself. The stroke had left him paralyzed on his left side: the left arm didn't move at all and the leg only barely so. Still, through a militaristic regime of diet and exercise, my father began walking with the use of a cane. Then he returned to his garden, at first just a few plants and animals, eventually a small suburban farm, with crops of squash, potatoes, corn, tomatoes, onions, strawberries, basil, and oregano, and livestock including a goat, chickens, pigeons, and rabbits. Despite his handicap, he struggled on with the only thing that calmed him: meaningful work. My parents sowed, tilled, slaughtered, and watered together, just as they had at Zio Carmine's. When the time came to dismantle his backyard kingdom, the debris weighed more than thirteen tons—one for each year since his stroke. I was away at graduate school when my family took it all down. When I came home and saw the pristine green patch where my father's miniature farm had once stood, I broke down. His southern Italian footprint had been wiped off the map of New England.

In season two of *The Sopranos*, Tony and the boys return to Naples for business. Their resale of stolen cars has been suffering because Uncle Junior trusted the wrong fences in Brooklyn: Russians and other East Europeans have been skimming off profits. Tony decides to keep the matter in the family and hire Italian middlemen to peddle his stolen Mercedes SUVs in Europe. Where better to look than in his ancestral home? "This is the real thing," Paulie announces as they arrive in sun-drenched Naples. Christopher promises to hit the topless beaches and "see that fucking crater," Mount Vesuvius, though his heroin addiction will keep him sequestered in a hotel room for the entire trip. Paulie goes native. "Tone, try this octopus," he says at an elegant dinner with local Mob heads. For Paulie, the Neapolitan homecoming is epochal, though some of the customs—and the nasty public restrooms—perplex him. He asks for "gravy" (tomato sauce) on his "macaroni" (spaghetti) instead of the local squid ink, a request that leads his Neapolitan counterpart to comment to his boss, "And you thought the Germans were classless pieces of shit."

The contrast between Italy as an idea and a reality colors Tony's encounters with Neapolitan culture. When the curvaceous wife of the local *capo*, Annalisa, takes Tony to the Sibyl at Cumae, she rehearses a scene that has taken place for centuries: the pilgrimage of an Italian cultural enthusiast to an ancient site. Before you, she tells Tony, the Romans were here, before them the Greeks, and so on. Tony Soprano, the ultimate

alpha male, shrinks before our eyes. She asks him if he wants
her, and he says no mixing business and pleasure ("I don't
shit where I eat"). Instead, they conclude their deal: the Italians will get the cars for $75,000 each, and Tony will get
Annalisa's trusted soldier Furio in return.

What does Tony see at Cumae? Very little, for his connection to the Old Country withered long before his arrival in
Naples. He acts and thinks like an official "Italian American" in the basest sense, with his yacht *The Stugots* (dialect for
Questo Cazzo, literally, "This Prick," but also a general expression of disgust). And he is as oblivious of the real Italy as
Paulie, with his romantic notions of ancestral ties (Paulie and
the prostitute he hires turn out to be from the same neighborhood, a coincidence that excites him but bores her). Tony
is as jaded as the prostitute. "How's Italy?" his wife, Carmela,
asks him early in his stay. "Pretty friggin' good," he says, for
he eats well in the homeland and, all things considered, the
trip is a success. But Italy itself remains, for Tony and countless others who have sat in its gondolas and stared at its art,
more an idea than an actual place.

When Tony, Christopher, and Paulie return to New Jersey from Naples, the translucent blue of the Neapolitan sky
cedes to the industrial wasteland surrounding Newark International. Pussy asks them how the trip went, and Paulie
answers, "Fabulous. I felt right at home," adding his name to
Goethe, Shelley, the Brownings, and many other foreigners
who have sought their own private Italy. "Give me your tired,
your poor, your huddled masses," Emma Lazarus has the
American Statue of Liberty proclaim, her lines suggesting
the future rewards that toil, luck, and upward mobility unre-
stricted by class or blood can bring. In Italy, the vectors are

the opposite. Foreigners travel there to look backward, to live in a land surrounded by the ruins of history and emblems of the past. But it's hard to build a home on an idea. Christopher never does visit the topless beaches or Vesuvius, nor does he buy his girlfriend Adriana the Italian gifts he had promised her. He has to settle for something from Fendi in the airport duty-free shop. The gift will carry the label MADE IN ITALY, and Adriana will never know the difference. Just like the millions of tourists each year who see the exact replicas of Michelangelo's *David* in Florence, she will have a tough time telling the original from the knockoffs.

Years after my father's stroke, I came home unannounced from graduate school on a summer day to visit my parents. The backyard led to a wooded area that provided a welcome breeze in summer, and my parents often relaxed there in the afternoon. It was lunchtime, and I could smell the fumes of meat as I descended the cement path toward them. They were chatting about this and that, and my mother was cutting my father's meat, pouring his wine, and scurrying back and forth to replenish his plate from the grill. The intimacy was as thick as fog. I had never caught my parents "in the act"— except for one embarrassed Saturday evening as a teenager, when I was shocked to see that they had climbed into the same bed after a party. Though I was accustomed to their cries of accusation and resentment, this backyard gentleness was alien. Endurance was the cardinal virtue of their union, which began just after Mussolini and ended with Clinton. But on that steamy July day I saw that part of their connection

had nothing to do with providing for their children or playing out ancient family roles. They were tender with each
other, and they were alone—no children, no threat from a
German officer or the caress of a German wife, no unpaid bill
lying on the table. They were as intertwined as the roots of
the towering oak beneath their picnic table.

Around the time I surprised them in the backyard, I met
my parents in the least private of places, New York City, for
the festival of the patron saint of our Calabrian village, the
Beato Angelo. With his leathery skin and crisply ironed ox-
ford shirt, my father looked like what he was: a farmer come
to the big city for the annual fair. My mother wore her finest
blue dress, with her hair up, and the two of them appeared
to have been transported by a time machine from postwar
Calabria to postmodern Manhattan. We navigated the fake
jewelry and leather bags splayed out on Canal Street and
arrived for lunch in Little Italy. I had gnocchi, and we all
drank red wine. As we ate and reminisced, I couldn't help
thinking that they didn't belong here—not just in bustling
downtown New York but in this enormous new country,
some four thousand miles from the mountains and fields where
they had met. I walked with my mother to a bakery after
lunch and took her by the arm for the first time in my life.

My mother once said something that struck me with a
force like that of no other words I can recall: during my
father's courtship and afterward in the first ten years of their
marriage in Italy, he had been . . . happy. Even carefree. I have
many memories of my father. In some of them he is exuber-
ant, even ecstatic; in many he is troubled to the point of tor-
ture. But after my mother's words I could picture him back
in 1946, in the fields of Calabria, surrounded by mountains.

Beside him, my uncle Giorgio holds a harmonica, and a bottle of wine lies on the ground between them. The nighttime sky, the young woman he loves and has decided to marry—all of this fills him. He is alive somehow, though he has seen the most frightening things imaginable in Germany, though he himself had been called to death at least twice there. My dad is singing, serenading his wife-to-be. He doesn't know that in ten years he will leave this beautiful land, that he will set out for something that will require immense determination and self-denial. His children will bear the fruits of his labor, and he will never cease to remind them that their freedom has cost him his happiness—though he won't use words to convey this. His broken body will be enough to signal it. But there, on a summer night in Calabria in 1946, he has music, wine, and stars.

Neither of my parents showed a particular interest in my study of Italian until I went to Yale—and only then because the name of the school, like Nike or Coca-Cola, was instantly recognizable. By the time I was in graduate school, my father began to accept my choice of career. Then one day he announced that he was going to give me some of the money that he had spent his lifetime saving.

"Be careful," he said, as he handed me a fat check. "*'N trattara cu gende maddamente,*" "Stay away from people who are sick in the head. And come to me if you ever need anything."

I had never heard him speak this way before. That summer, he said, was the last that he was going to tend his garden.

During his final trip to Italy, the year he and my mother went to claim the inheritance left to them by Zio Carmine and Zia Rosaria, they stopped in Rome on the way to Calabria. They took a carriage ride, and in my mind's eye they seem as out of place there as they had been that day in New York when they went to worship the Beato Angelo. All told, the estate of my grandparents Carmine and Rosaria Crocco was about $9,000, a decent amount for that part of the world at that time, and the sum total of all those years of collecting rents on their now-vanished properties. Some of the money was used to pay for the education that culminated in my Ph.D.

The Italian culture I studied at Yale and that of my parents were from two separate worlds. But in the end, all three of us were Italian exiles: my parents, disconnected from a homeland they gave up at the start of their adult lives; me, spending my adult life pursuing an Italy they had never known. My father kept his distance from American culture his entire life: no HBO, no posters on my bedroom wall, no free expression in our house. My mother issued no such edicts. But when she said *u miu paisu*, "my country," the place she was referring to was never in doubt: it was Calabria, not Italy. For all our love, for all the blood we shared, my parents and I belonged to two separate *paesi*.

I wonder what went through Zio Carmine's mind that day when he found out that my father might have raped his daughter. And I wonder what my grandmother Rosaria felt when my father swore to her that he didn't lay a finger on my mother, that he just wanted to frighten her. All it would have taken, from either of them, was a tremor of suspicion, a cold word to their daughter, and the wedding would have been canceled, my father would have been carted off to jail, and my mother would have been handed over to that gentle soul in the neighboring village who said he'd still have her, scarlet letter and all. I don't know whether it was destiny or love or luck that sealed my father and mother's fate—and by extension my own—all those years ago in Italy, but I do believe that Pasquale Luzzi and Yolanda Crocco knew from the moment they met that there was one and only one person for them, and that they would bear this burden for the rest of their lives.

2

Blood Pudding

At the end of the week I like to gather the aging vegetables in our fridge. I work my way through the dried-out onions and garlic, withered sprigs of parsley and thyme, piles of lumpy sweet potatoes, and finally the star vegetable, a massive head of red cabbage. It takes an hour to chop up everything, using all the available surface space in the kitchen. Then, four burners working overtime, the cooking requires another hour. The dish is one I never even heard of growing up; it now brings me closer to my family than anything else I eat.

Ribollita, or "reboiled" stew, is a Tuscan peasant dish made from food awaiting disposal. Chopping the onions, I picture my mother cooking them with liver, dousing the pan in sputtering vegetable oil that coated the stove with a light brown glaze. Adding the potato, I remember masses of this vegetable spread out by the barrowful on the floor of an unfinished cellar room where my dad fermented his wine and cured his prosciutto and soppressata (sausage consisting of the "suppressed," discarded elements of a slaughtered pig). Tomatoes, which we harvested by the bucketful, bring to mind the end of summer, when my parents' beefsteaks ripened into enormous red and yellow bulbs. I would slice their soft meat into wedges, add salt, then place them on slabs of my mom's homemade bread. On a visit of mine to Calabria, my cousin Giuseppe stopped in his garden, plucked a late-summer gem from the vine, and ate it on the spot, as if he were out apple picking. The tomato nearly burst from all its life in the southern Italian sun. I realized then, for the first time, that a tomato truly is a fruit and not a vegetable.

My mother would boil the signature vegetable of ribollita, red cabbage (*u cappucciu*, the "hooded" vegetable), in large cauldrons and serve it unadorned as a soggy *contorno*, "side dish," that my father adored and I abhorred. She baked bread, another ingredient of ribollita, in loaves by the dozens, in all shapes and sizes: flat, dense disks perfect for stuffing with steak, provolone, and onions; doughy clouds that released billows of smoke when ripped into as they were taken fresh from the oven; and industrial-sized loaves of indeterminate shape created without art and intended for immediate consumption. This last group, the ugliest, tasted best.

When I make ribollita, I remember above all the energy conservation that defined my parents' household. The dish's economical nature would have pleased my father, a man who recycled the aluminum foil of his lunch sandwiches—and not because he cared about the environment. His salary peaked at about $15,000 a year in 1982, and he had six children. Yet somehow he managed to save $100,000 and purchase three parcels of land after those twenty-five years of factory work. Because he had no checkbook, my mother went around to the various utility offices to pay our bills in cash. In 1967, when he purchased a Chevy Impala for $3,000, he also paid cash up front at the dealership and drove the car off the lot. He grew his own food, from peas and pears to corn and cabbage; and he raised his own livestock, including chickens, pigeons, rabbits, and a goat. He and my mother preserved everything from tomatoes and beans to peaches and pears in rows of mason jars that filled the cellar alongside the hanging shanks of prosciutto and soppressata.

Ribollita transforms potential waste into a hearty vegetable stew that holds for weeks and tastes better over time: the flavors and spices soak the bread and come to life when mixed with a dollop of olive oil. Likewise, my parents wasted nothing, transforming the earth around our home into what I now realize was boutique food at a bargain rate. My parents didn't pursue a farm-to-table lifestyle because they were foodies; they did so out of necessity. For this reason my mother never understood why I would choose, when there was abundant frozen or prepared food at hand, to make something as labor-intensive as ribollita. *"Ma perché ti curì i causti?"* she would ask in Calabrian. "But why saddle your shoulders?"

Making ribollita brings back my earliest memories. In the early 1970s, while suburban families flocked to the frozen-food section for their Swanson and Sara Lee, my parents harvested the land and husbanded the animals by hand, not a single tractor or engine on-site. I remember standing while still a toddler beside my mother, who was wearing a blue duffel jacket and carrying a pail of potato skins. She held my hand and led me down a long hill that sloped toward a shed. I waddled alongside her until we reached a rusted structure, the family barn, where my mother unhinged the locks. Inside, a creature, so enormous that its pink skin filled the entire barn, sat immobile. I don't remember being afraid, but I was awed by the sheer bulk of the animal. I can still picture the horrid face gazing out with no direction, its satisfaction in life reduced to an immovable feast of dirty peelings.

Soon afterward my father's friend Giuseppe Gencarelli fired his shotgun into the pig's skull. Then they hoisted its lifeless body up a makeshift pole in our backyard, on that same slope leading to the shed. Once the beast was airborne, a team of Calabrian butchers reduced the pig to vapors. They quartered the legs so that the succulent hind meat could be cured into *prosciutto crudo*, the Calabrian version of which is much saltier than the sweet *prosciutto di Parma* that most American restaurants and gourmet grocers serve. Then they divided the belly and midsection into parcels of meat for our relatives. Most coveted and succulent of all were the ribs, their moist fat barely clinging to the bone. The leftover parts would be turned into soppressata. Finally, the pig's innards were removed and pickled in a jelly called *zuzzu*, a concoction that, even among these hearty eaters, repelled all but the most cast iron of stomachs. My father reserved the head for himself—droit du seigneur—and would relish the eyes, crunching their membranes with slow chews at some later meal.

Even the blood was drained into a viscous pudding. Although this dish has now become the darling of foodies, I can't face it without revulsion. The reduction of a pig's physical essence and vital fluid—I won't say its soul—to a cake of maroon liquid struck me as beyond cruel. At least the other dishes that came from the dead animal were messy enough to recall the living, breathing form that made them possible. But the blood pudding, a perfect circular distillation that hinted at no hairy hoof or pink nose, hid its source. Its innocuous presentation—a reminder of all the custards, puddings, and sundaes I lived for—masked a lethal efficiency.

I was too young to remember this first ritual slaughter, but I would soon witness my share of others, and not just of pigs. The goats haunted me the most. There was no rhyme or reason to how my father dispatched them. There was always a crew of relatives on hand, and as with the pigs, the beast would be repurposed to its last millimeter of flesh. The crew of butchers set receptacles in place before the killing to make sure that not a drop of blood spilled on the grass. One time, two men subdued the goat while my father bludgeoned it with a hammer, four quick blows to the skull that sent me sprawling on my bedroom floor in tears as I watched from a window. At another slaughter, to me the most vicious of all, the goat was hung upside down from a tree while my father slid a long knife into its neck. I had never felt the hiss of that word *slid* until I watched the knife divide the soft flesh. The blood and life oozed out of the animal as quietly as the knife had entered it. All the while, my mother stood by her man, an infernal nurse who helped chop, process, and package the tissue and innards into whatever bottle, pan, or bucket was needed. None of them, not my father, not Giuseppe Gencarelli nor my mother, expressed the slightest emotion during any of this. They were merely ancient rituals.

I despised them for their murderous indifference. What kind of man, I wondered, could deliver four crunching blows to the head of an innocent animal without a blink? Who could slash the throat of another creature with no hint of remorse? And my mother, standing by grimly, even a bit bored—was she any better?

My parents may have seemed cold, cruel even, in dispatching the animals we ate. But they did more than slaughter their victims: they had also nurtured them. They fed, sheltered, and cared for almost all the animals they butchered. If you're an animal destined for the dinner table, where better to spend your days than in the suburbs of Rhode Island, the ocean breeze in your maw on a quaint, family-run farm? While the rest of their species suffered anonymously in industrial cages and suffocating stalls, the Luzzi beasts enjoyed an aristocratic, free-range existence. Any death delivered by my mother's or father's hand was done with honor and respect, for they made use of every particle that had animated the creature.

Though I didn't realize it, my family had perfected the art of slow food.

Italians are renowned for the down-to-earth deliciousness of their largely peasant and local cooking traditions. You don't need a Cordon Bleu certification, Le Creuset pots and pans, Wüsthof knives, or a Viking range to prepare food Italian-style. In a nation of divisions, Italian food offers a unifying blast of oven heat. But its aromas differ from one region to the next. The Sicilian accent and dialect are unintelligible to a Turinese; so too does the Ligurian pesto confound a Neapolitan used to lathering his pasta in tomato sauce or squid ink. The rosy Calabrian soppressata looks and tastes nothing like the brunette Germanic würstel of Friuli. The eggplant Parmesan in Puglia is tinged a soft maroon, the Milanese version a crisp light brown, with not a hint of red—or tomato—to be found. Tuscan food, from crostini and ribollita to such local vegetables as olives and porcini mushrooms, tends toward the brown and salt-free, while Venetian cuisine dances in saffron and other bold-colored spices. And not all Italians are pasta-mad: a *primo* in Tuscany is just as likely to be *pappa al pomodoro*, a tomato and bread soup, as lasagne or spaghetti. Many dishes, like certain words, do not translate from one region to the next. The base of Tuscan ribollita is a local ingredient difficult to grow in other Italian soil, *cavolo nero*, "black cabbage." You can make it, as I do and must, with red cabbage. But then you're eating in translation, just like reading *The Divine Comedy* in a language other than Italian. The deracinated version is still tasty; it's just not the real thing.

Dante uses food to embody one of the most poignant moments in his entire poem. The reader has known since early on in the *Inferno* that Dante will be exiled, as characters that the poet meets in hell hint at the awful fate awaiting him. But it isn't until the *Paradiso* that we get an explicit description of Dante's banishment, when his ancestor Cacciaguida predicts Dante's exile in the most flavorful of terms:

> 'You shall leave behind all you most dearly love,
> and that shall be the arrow
> first loosed from exile's bow.
> 'You shall learn how [salty] is the taste
> of another man's bread and how hard is the way,
> going down and then up another man's stairs.'

Dante's exile would indeed be one of bitter tastes—and Cacciaguida isn't just speaking metaphorically. As visitors to Florence know, Florentines make their bread without salt.

Some have linked the city's *sciocco*, "insipid" or "salt-free," bread to this historical fact: in the twelfth century, Florence was forced to obtain the costly salt product through commerce with its mortal enemy, Pisa. Pisa eventually blocked its sale of salt to Florence for political reasons, so the Florentines learned to make do without. The Florentines even have the expression *"Meglio un morto in casa che un pisano all'uscio"* ("Better a dead person in the house than a Pisan on the doorstep"). So when Dante, who also despised the Pisans, writes that exile will teach him how salty the bread at others' tables would be, he conjures up the strange food he will be forced to consume far from home. The Tuscan culinary genius extends to something that in America we are accustomed to throwing out: stale bread. Ribollita and *pappa al pomodoro* join such staples as *panzanella* (a salad mixed with moist bread), *zuppa di cavolo*, "cabbage soup," and *zuppa di pane* ("bread soup" with hot broth and grated Parmesan) to make Tuscan one of Italy's most ecologically minded cuisines.

Any mention of the word *ecology* in conjunction with food is likely to evoke the name of Carlo Petrini. A native of the renowned food and wine region of Piedmont, Petrini founded a movement called Slow Food in 1986, and since then he has become an international spokesman for the conservationist aspect of Italian cuisine. The acclaimed American chef Alice Waters writes that under Petrini's leadership, "Slow Food has become a standard bearer against the fast-food values that threaten to homogenize and industrialize our food heritge . . . Slow food reminds us that food is more than fuel to be consumed as quickly as possible and that, like anything worth doing, eating takes *time*."

For Petrini, Slow Food is not just the title of a book or the name of a movement; it reflects the conviction that eating should be an enjoyable experience consisting of varied, healthy, and flavorful food—the opposite of fast food. "The Official Slow Food Manifesto" argues that the twentieth century, "which began and has developed under the insignia of industrial civilization, first invented the machine and then took it as its life model." The ascendancy of "speed," along with what Petrini calls "Fast Life," now "disrupts our habits, pervades the privacy of our homes and forces us to eat Fast Foods." According to Petrini, "a firm defense of quiet material pleasure is the only way to oppose the universal folly of *Fast Life*."

For many years, the United States and its mass-produced junk food was Petrini's public enemy number one. Yet his international movement has grown with more speed and force in the United States than anywhere else. In 2008 Kim Severson wrote in *The New York Times* that Petrini's Slow Food "has a tendency to polarize people," and that while many Americans were drawn to its philosophy, others were put off by what they saw as its elitism and self-importance. In a similar vein, critics believe that Slow Food is too ideological (it is leftist); has Luddite, antitechnological biases; is antiglobalization; and, above all, fails to communicate its message to the "average person." It's been thought of as haute food philosophy for the chattering classes. Still, there is no denying the reach of the Slow Food movement, which now has more than 100,000 members in 153 countries.

I met Petrini in 2012, when he appeared at the Italian Cultural Institute in New York. Scores of students, likely former acolytes at the University of Gastronomic Sciences in Piedmont, founded by Petrini in 2004, had come for what

was advertised as an "encounter" with Petrini and his principle of "slowness." In the audience, Italian leather jackets and
hip-hugging skirts mingled with precision-ripped jeans and
manicured nails—you could have mistaken the public lecture for a SoHo art opening. Cultural attachés and captains
of industry chatted with undergraduates and professors; Isa-
bella Rossellini sat quietly in the back. Petrini spoke for an
hour, sticking to his maxims of deceleration and fair trade.

During our interview after his talk Petrini stressed that
food is not simply a portal to pleasure; it is part of the network of social obligations that constitutes a meaningful life.

"Pleasure is fundamental to Slow Food," he said, "but only
when it goes hand in hand with responsibility. The subtitle
to Slow Food when it was born was 'international movement for the protection of and right to pleasure.'" He added,
"If the protection of and right to pleasure isn't shared, if it is
egotistical, it is not pleasure."

When I pressed him about the charge that Slow Food
has been labeled as elitist, he admitted that this criticism had
plagued the group from the beginning, but in his view it was
misguided. Once again he explained the misunderstanding
through the notion of pleasure: "Many would actually like
Slow Food to be a rigorous force for social change, without
an emphasis on pleasure. We say, instead, that pleasure is a
right. How to share pleasure is a difficult question. Because I
don't believe in the need to create niche products, which are
only for those with money. I believe in the right to quality
for all."

I asked Petrini if there was something specifically "Italian"
about Slow Food, but he demurred. "I feel more a citizen
of the world," he said, warning against the chauvinism that

could mar the movement if it was seen as exclusively *italiano*. I heard Petrini's strong Piedmont accent come through as he was trying to distance himself from his local roots. I couldn't help thinking about the similar phrase Dante used in his language treatise, *De vulgari eloquentia* (*On Eloquence in the Vernacular*, c. 1304–1305): "The whole world is [my] homeland, like the sea to fish," he wrote, just before adding a massive qualifier, "though I drank from the Arno before cutting my teeth, and love Florence so much that [it has caused me to] suffer exile unjustly."

Petrini, like Dante, had to profess the universality of his program, no matter how intensely he felt the pull of his hometown, his region, his country. Slow Food is an international movement, a mantra even, for those dedicated to linking the enjoyment of their daily bread with moral, political, and social causes. The "slow food" I had in mind, however, was less diplomatic. I was trying to understand how certain types of food shaped me and created the culture I loved. The symbol of Petrini's Slow Food movement is a snail. But I remained fixated on the slaughtered pig.

Dante's nostalgia for Tuscan bread revealed how inseparable his idea of Florence was from the foods he had eaten there. And as the child of Italian immigrants, I saw how difficult it was for my parents to let go of Calabrian cuisine. From the animals our family raised to the foods we cured, the aromas and tastes of my parents' abandoned region continued to permeate their lives. This seemed natural enough to me as a child, but as I got older, I noticed that Italian food exerted a

similar emotional pull on people—both actual and invented—
who had no roots in the Old Country.

On his last night in Rome before returning to New York,
Lenny Abramov, the protagonist of Gary Shteyngart's *Super
Sad True Love Story*, enjoys a farewell meal with the young
Korean woman he has just fallen for; they are in a restaurant
favored by theater actors:

> Enormous plates of food were needed to mop up this
> overindulgence [of ours in wine]. We thoughtfully
> chewed on the pig jowls of the *bucatini all'amatriciana*,
> slurped up a plate of spaghetti with spicy eggplant, and
> picked apart a rabbit practically drowning in olive oil.
> I knew I would miss all this when I got back to New
> York.

A farce about a dystopian world where emails and electronic
devices have replaced books and human interaction, Shteyngart's Rome—its Pantheon, his Italian lover with "her curves
fixed by carbohydrates"—symbolizes the "Old World and
its dying nonelectronic corporeality." Especially the carbs.
Back in America, Lenny finds a youth-obsessed culture terrified of putting on weight and wary of starches and other
vestiges of Italian cuisine. The postmodern world is no place
to wait for a three-hour *ragù* to thicken.

In the novel, the word *Italy* becomes a code for the Western past, and the foods consumed there represent a diet from
a lost time. On a recent visit to Rome, I spoke with many
people connected to the Italian culinary scene and movements
like Slow Food. The foreigners I met discussed such local Roman dishes as *cacio e pepe* (a pasta dish with black pepper and

pecorino cheese) and *carciofi alla giudia* ("Jewish-style" deep-fried artichokes) with the reverence reserved for Caravaggio's paintings and Bernini's sculpture. Tourists built their days around the local fare: the richest espresso and creamiest brioche in the morning; the tangiest *amatriciana* at noon; the most savory ossobuco and most suggestive *vino rosso* for dinner. It isn't enough to devour these riches—they need to be analyzed and described, the more lyrically the better.

I added my voice to the chorus, but not without a nagging sense of hypocrisy. As a kid, I had scorned all that home-made freshness, desperate for the packaged and processed, the fructose and trans fat that would help me fit in. Though my childhood was filled with organic produce and freshly butchered livestock, by my teenage years I was obsessed with eating American. In the first years of high school, I would sit in the cafeteria and tear open the aluminum foil packaging in my bag, releasing the smell of fried peppers and eggs among my straight-haired classmates and their odorless peanut-butter-and-jelly sandwiches. I squirmed as the oil seeped through the bag and onto my fingers. When my mother had prepared the pepper and egg in the morning, it was warm to the touch, another cozy ingredient in our tidy home. But by lunchtime it felt like cold rubber on my tongue, and its drippings made the crusty homemade bread soggy. Later at home I begged my mother to give me a bland lunch just like that of the other kids. I eventually wore her down and was allowed to pack the same grilled cheeses and Hostess cakes as everyone else. All around me, Tater Tots and fish sticks welcomed me to America.

We consecrated every event in our home with some dish. On Christmas Eve I would force down the *baccalà* (salted cod) and the six other fish dishes that my red-meat family otherwise snubbed as I waited for my father's return from his annual holiday cocktail next door at the Pfalzengraffs, a German-Italian family blessed with two voluptuous teenage girls who walked me to school. I dreamed of stealing a moment under the mistletoe with plush Arabella while my siblings devoured plate after plate of linguini with calamari, *spaghetti alle vongole*, and, worst of all, stuffed shrimp, an American concoction that had never graced a Calabrian table. Soon enough we would hear my father's footsteps. We hoped he had won a peck from Arabella or her equally curvy sister, Karin— anything to calm him down during the messy unwrapping of the gifts, the ritual that awoke his inner Mussolini.

Thanksgiving brought its own culinary perils. With its pasta and turkey, soppressata and stuffing, fried dough and pumpkin pie, our table was too much of a mishmash for anyone to take seriously. My father would be on his best behavior—too subdued, really. He didn't understand Thanks- giving, had no knowledge of the Pilgrims, their dissent against the Anglican Church, their first long winters in places like Boston and nearby Providence.

"Just imagine," my eleventh-grade English teacher, Mr. Weiss, would say, "what it was like to endure a New England winter . . . with no indoor heating."

A squat man with a nasal voice, Mr. Weiss used such phrases as "morsel of feminine pulchritude" and pronounced the *u* in *puma* in the British style (PEW-ma), affectations that earned him enormous prestige at my high school. We could all picture those earliest Americans chattering in bed. But my father worshipped neither the Puritans' God nor the nation they helped create. Dressed in his rust-colored holiday cords and pine sweater vest, he went through the Thanks-giving motions, helping himself to dollops of cranberry sauce in a rare sign of assimilation to his adopted country.

Christenings and weddings meant *currarille*, a braided dough that my father deep-fried, with the aid of a tree branch, in a ten-gallon vat of vegetable oil; *bucanotti*, "holes in the night," a jam-filled pastry with powdered sugar; and the famous *pitte fritte*, more deep-fried dough, the dessert version covered with sugar and butter.

As scented and savory as all this was, I was convinced it was beneath me, that I belonged in a world beyond fried dough and cured meat. When I started college, I left not only my family but also their refrigerator, garden, and cellar. My first date with someone out of my league—and dietary habitat—was a junior with a pageboy haircut and a major street named after her colonial family on Brown's campus in Providence. She had spent her teenage years in Paris and spoke noncha-lantly about all the casual sex she had enjoyed there, deepening my awe of her. She took me to a venerable Boston seafood house, where I ate scallops for the first time in my life. I picked up the tab to impress her (forty-eight financial-aid-free dol-lars), and later we made out furiously in front of her apartment before she brushed me aside and rushed upstairs. Soon after, she took me to a sushi restaurant in Somerville, and I felt like I was falling in love—not so much with my gorgeous date, but with her impeccable Yankee pedigree and the ocean of new flavors she was introducing me to. A week or so later, after a series of unreturned phone calls, I found out that she had left campus for an impromptu study abroad program. I would miss her girlish refinement, but was eternally grateful: she had condescended to share her menu with me.

The only subject I studied faithfully in college was food. As a southern Italian male teenager, I wasn't allowed to touch anything in the kitchen at home. In college, with its dinner parties and ethnic restaurants, I familiarized myself with the zests, spices, and mandolines that propelled me into a new world of taste. My mother was always shocked to learn that I would *willingly* cook dinner for friends or a girlfriend. And she was wary of any woman who would let a man sink to such depths of gender betrayal.

"All they want to know about is going out and restaurants," she would comment ominously before suggesting the inevitable result with a *"statti accortu"* ("watch yourself"). This was the closest we ever came to discussing the facts of life.

Despite my mother's best efforts, I developed an instinctive feel for how much broth to add to a risotto to keep the grains al dente, or why Parmesan cheese would ruin the tastiest scallop. I never measured and always worked by feel, especially when it came to sauces, stews, and other slow-cook fare. I learned this not from my mother, but from my father. I had never seen him cook a thing, other than baking potatoes by burying them at the base of a bonfire when he cleared brush. But his sense of the material world—how to pick a vegetable, prune a hedge, or sever the head of a chicken—shaped my muscle memory as I mastered a growing catalog of dishes.

Meanwhile, I sought to quash the ethnic traditions that had nourished me. I boasted to my new college friends that "my parents and older siblings were all born in Italy." Technically, this was not a lie, but certainly a violation in spirit. When it came to food, among other things, my parents remained steadfastly Calabrian. A Piedmontese classic like *bagna càuda* or a slice of Roman saltimbocca was more foreign to them than a burger and fries washed down with a liter of Coke.

The longer my parents spent in the United States, the more entrenched their eating habits became. The table was the one place where my father could truly remain himself. He had been forced, because of immigration, to leave his job in the fields under the Calabrian sun for the inside of a factory. But come dinnertime, he and my mother could re-create their lost world. She served him plate after plate of the past—not first course, second course, dessert, and coffee, as in Italy, but all at once, American and Calabrian peasant–style. There was the obligatory pasta dish, usually the long, pierced bucatini with tomato sauce; there was meat, also stewed in tomato and in a wealth of forms (beef, goat, pigeon), perhaps even white meat. An array of vegetables accompanied the feast—beans, cabbage, peas, corn, or broccoli—along with brimming flasks of his own homemade wine. All the produce, and much of the meat, came from his garden. All of it, from the chicken feet and goat eyeballs to the boiled cabbage and stewed fava beans, was the same food he had eaten in Calabria. Every day from five to seven p.m., perched at the head of the table, my father consumed the only American things he had a genuine grasp of—the food that reminded him of his lost homeland. There's an Italian expression, *a tavola non s'invecchia mai*, "one never grows old at the table"—because time there is suspended. My father was indeed growing old in America, despite those wine-soaked interludes where he could enjoy the illusion of being at home in his adopted country. No wonder he often fell asleep in that dining room chair, his face contorted by snores and obscured by cigarette smoke.

During the later years of my father's dinnertime regime I visited Calabria with my younger sister, who, like me, was born in the United States. Shortly after we arrived, my cousin

Giuseppe Gabriele picked us up in his blue BMW—apparently, the gas station he owned was booming—and drove us through the hills outside Cosenza to the house of his father-in-law, who was nicknamed *il Conte*, "the Count," because of his lordly manor and extensive properties. It was a mild December day, and we were far from any industry or pollution. The air felt thick and clear enough to drink.

The day revolved around a feast, as the Count had slaughtered one of his prize pigs. A group had come earlier to dispatch the beast, and mercifully, the bloodiest work was completed by the time we arrived. While I walked the property and surveyed the cloudless skies, busy Calabrian hands drew and quartered, flayed and shaved, reducing the beast to its constituent parts. All my cousin Giuseppe could talk about was *u suffrittu* (*il soffritto*, a "lightly fried" pork dish to be made from the fresh kill). The classic *soffritto* consists of garlic, onions, carrots, celery, salt, and pepper sautéed in olive oil as a base for sauces. By contrast, in Calabria the dish is an end in itself, and it involves cooking meat in tomato sauce, onion, celery, and abundant red pepper. Giuseppe's eyes widened as he described it. He had Zia Filomena's blue eyes and, like many Calabrian men, kept the nail on his pinkie long. The Count bottled his own sparkling white wine. It was exquisite, and Giuseppe drank more than his share, leaving me to worry about how he would handle the winding nighttime hills on our drive back. The slaughtered pig was cut in two; then a juicy extract from the neck was removed and cooked in a *suffrittu* of parsley, basil, tomato, and olive oil.

We spent the evening in the Count's kitchen, drinking his bubbly and dining on slabs of *suffrittu*. I had never tasted meat so fresh and could feel the life of the animal as I chewed.

I was four thousand miles from my childhood backyard, that first leviathan was long since dead and digested, yet I felt connected to my first house, the parents that nurtured me there, the beasts that provided our sustenance. Cut off from the world in the heights of Cosenza and filled with chilled white wine and stewed pork, there was nothing to do but listen to the quiet of the hills. Maybe that's what I was doing that winter day in the 1970s as I followed my mother down the long slope to the hungry pig, when I lived in fear of the blood pudding. Filled with *suffrittu* at the Count's table, I felt the animal's transformation; as a young boy staring at a cake of maroon blood, I could only imagine its disappearance.

During my recent visit to Rome I spent the day working as a volunteer in the kitchen of the American Academy, where I was a visiting scholar. After preparing and serving lunch, a group of kitchen workers and I gathered to butcher a suckling pig. Snout to hoof, the beast was no more than two feet long and had come to us already slaughtered. The innards had been hollowed, and the head chef began the process of "breaking down" the animal, which would be served as porchetta, a classic, fatty Roman dish of boneless pork roast. The pig would first have to be gutted, deboned, and reconstituted into layers of stuffing, meat, fat, and skin, which would then be rolled and spit-roasted over wood in the traditional style. Recipes vary, but the dish is usually salted and leavened with garlic, rosemary, sage, fennel, and other herbs. The slow cooking makes the skin extremely crispy—according to Chef Chris, "like glass."

He began the demonstration by scoring the pig along
the spine to flatten out the right and left flaps of meat and
prevent the animal from lolling around the cutting board.
As I stared into the face of the dead animal, I tried to recall
the pigs of my childhood, but the line was broken. This tiny
creature was beyond gone: he looked more like food than
an animal. As the chef's knife pared, pruned, trimmed, and
probed, the pig's head was thrown back in seeming anguish,
its grimace and eyeless sockets suggesting an unhappy de-
mise. For us, his butchers, the entire process hung on the
deboning. Its legs removed one at a time, the pig came to
resemble an envelope of meat.

"We need to follow the reticulum road," Chef Chris
remarked as he guided his blade along the fatty material separating the muscle tissue.

Slowly the meat unhinged in slabs, starting with the ribs.
We preserved the integrity of the legs; we made sure that no
bone shard contaminated the meat; we strategized about the
hip bones and neck socket. Then it was my turn to wield the
knife. As the date of my volunteer duty approached, I had
wondered if I'd be able to handle the sight, the smell, and
above all the feel of the roseate muscle and tissue. After all,
growing up, I had witnessed the horrific carnage, by my own
father no less, of countless animals, from the strangled chickens
and the assassinated rabbits to the elaborately choreographed
executions of pigs and goats. Now here I was, the grim killing done for me, charged with slicing up the suckling. I wondered if I would be up to it—if I was man enough. I knew
deep down that one of the things that made my father "a man"
was his capacity to kill. I don't know if he had to exercise that
function as a soldier in World War II, but I do know that in

the garden and the cellar, he could be a ruthless destroyer of life. Consciously, I feared him because of this; unconsciously, I was jealous.

Chef Chris handed me the blade. Summoning my deepest reservoir of *sprezzatura*, I set lightly to work. *Follow the reticulum road*, I whispered to myself. *Just go through the motions.* As my father, mother, and their helper Giuseppe Gencarelli had done amid all those carcasses. As my aunts and uncles had done while they slopped blood pudding on their plates and wiped the pickled pig jelly from their mouths. My knife worked the seam; my hands separated the fat from the pink tissue below it. It was cool and smooth to the touch. And it was a homecoming. I felt none of the revulsion and squeamishness I had anticipated—only that this was honest work and that I could feel my father in my hands. The world of books, to which I had devoted myself, was foreign to him, and his own passion for planting, pruning, and harvesting was one I didn't share. But here, as I wielded the knife, I pictured his hands, though they were much coarser than mine, much more capable of administering life and death, and certainly much more nimble in executing the present task.

Occasionally glancing over or throwing a comment my way, Chef Chris and the other kitchen workers ambled around me as they scrubbed, hosed, and partitioned the kitchen. Lunch service was over, and the space needed to be prepped for dinner. Without hurrying, without resting, I finished carving out my allotted section of the suckling. I was being casually ignored, the best a kitchen worker can hope for. With one hand on the muscle tissue and the other gripping the knife, I guided the blade along the reticulum.

PART II

LITTLE ITALIES

3

A Family Affair

On November 29, 2007, I lost my wife, Katherine Mester, suddenly, in a car accident. This book is not the place to dwell on this tragedy and the long season of grief and mourning that followed. It is enough to say that for a full year afterward, I needed an extraordinary amount of help, and not just to take care of myself. The day of my wife's death, she was eight and a half months pregnant. After an emergency cesarean, our daughter, Isabel, was born at eleven a.m.; Katherine died forty-five minutes later.

That first evening in the hospital, as the news of what had happened penetrated my shock, I thought, *Where will I go? What will I do?* My family was all around me in the neonatal unit of Vassar Brothers Medical Center in Poughkeepsie, where my four-pound, eight-ounce daughter incubated. I had slipped into a black hole and was hurtling into the darkness, wondering who or what could ever break my fall.

A month after the accident I moved back home to Rhode Island from New York and reclaimed my childhood bedroom.

My five siblings, all of whom live within a ten-minute drive from my mother, turned their lives upside down to help. My sister Mary used to go to the gym in the afternoon after work; she gave this up to visit Isabel and read to her or take her to the playground. Two other sisters, Margaret and Rose, took turns sleeping at my mother's place to assist her with Isabel when I needed to be away at work. My sister Tina, a working mother with two children of her own, changed her schedule to take Isabel to the beach, library, or playground. My brother, Angelo, checked in on Isabel and my mother every day, took them on errands, fixed anything that needed repairing, and helped me with the mountain of paperwork that accompanies an unexpected death. He told me which boxes to check, which lines to sign, which notices to respond to, and which ones to ignore.

Isabel's entry into the world was entirely arranged by her extended family. She played daily with her cousin and best friend, Michaela, age five, who lived next door, and she was taught how to ride a bike by her second cousin Rose, age seven, also a neighbor. Most heroically of all, my mother did the heavy lifting, nurturing Isabel while I kept time with the dead. While I slept in a fetal position in my childhood bed, my mother woke up at three a.m. to soothe my daughter's cries. She bathed her, disposed of her soiled diapers, burped her, and dried her tears. She filled her with the mother's love that had been taken away.

Slowly, I rejoined the living.

The bestseller *Outliers* by Malcolm Gladwell begins by describing a Pennsylvania mining town whose inhabitants experienced what one doctor called a "medical mystery." According to a report from 1965, in the community of Roseto, composed almost exclusively of Italian immigrants from its namesake town southeast of Rome, "virtually no one under 55 died of a heart attack, or showed any signs of heart disease. For men over 65, the death rate from heart disease in Roseto was roughly half that of the United States as a whole. The death rate from all causes in Roseto, in fact, was something like thirty or thirty-five percent lower than it should have been." The author of this medical report, Stewart Wolf, brought the sociologist John Bruhn with him to study the phenomenon. They soon discovered that it wasn't diet that had produced the healthy Rosetans, who consumed American-style pizza, cooked with lard, and ate lots of red meat. Wolf in fact found "that a whopping 41 percent of their calories came from fat." Nor were they type A personalities pounding the pavement in designer running shoes: exercise did not figure into the lives of most Rosetans, many of whom smoked heavily and struggled with obesity. And it wasn't genetics, either: the Rosetans who had immigrated to other parts of America had heart-disease rates in line with the national averages. Finally, location had little do with their health success. Other ethnic groups living in the area also experienced heart problems consistent with the national rates of incidence. More than just the mountain air was keeping these people healthy.

After extensive medical tests and interviews with the Rosetans, the two researchers concluded that the answer to the mystery lay in Roseto's way of life, social interactions, and cultural practices. Gladwell writes, "In transplanting the *paesani* culture of southern Italy to the hills of eastern Pennsylvania, the Rosetans had created a powerful, protective social

structure capable of insulating them from the pressures of
the modern world. The Rosetans were healthy because of
where they were *from*, because of the world they had created
for themselves in their tiny little town in the hills." The sociologist Bruhn was astonished to find the intergenerational
connections among the residents, something rare in the rest of
America: "I remember going to Roseto for the first time, and
you'd see three-generational family meals, all the bakeries,
the people walking up and down the street, sitting on their
porches talking to each other, the blouse mills where the
women worked during the day, while the men worked in
the slate quarries," Bruhn said. "It was magical."

Magical indeed.

   Two years after Katherine's accident I returned to Italy
and visited my friend Massimo, who hadn't seen me since
her death. I described to him how my family had come to
my rescue. We were standing in Florence's Piazza Santa Maria Novella, an elegant square tainted by its proximity to the
Fascist-era train station and the underground shopping mall
that joins the station to the *centro storico*. Not far from us, the
frescoes of Filippino Lippi and Domenico Ghirlandaio stood
inside the Basilica of Santa Maria Novella, founded by a Do-
minican order famous for its intellectual prowess, where every
day at dusk, flocks of starlings descend on a grove of trees
planted inside its walls. This black whir of wings and squawks
recalls Dante's celebrated lines about the sinners in *Inferno* 5,
driven here and there by the winds of lust: *"E come li stornei ne
portan l'ali / nel freddo tempo, a schiera larga e piena, / così quel fiato
li spiriti mali"* ("As, in cold weather, the wings of starlings / bear

them up in wide, dense flocks, / so does that blast propel the wicked spirits"). With his knotted scarf and long limbs, the aristocratic Massimo commanded the cobblestone square.

"*Guarda, Joseph,*" he said, "*è il genio della famiglia italiana.*"

Genio means "spirit," as in genius loci, the spirit a place exudes. But I also like to believe that it can mean the transliteration "genius." *Look, it's the spirit—the* genius—*of the Italian family.* The Italian family is like Italy itself: fragmented on the surface, riven by intrigue, resistant to change, suspicious of outsiders, and quick to set individual interests over group ones. Yet, like Italy, *la famiglia* has an overarching sense of identity that has withstood centuries of disunity, corruption, foreign occupation, and church intervention. For obvious reasons, my friend's words reminded me of the unexpected health benefits enjoyed by the Rosetans; less obviously, they recalled someone I hadn't thought about for years: Domenico Bellacqua, a close family friend and the center of a scandal that shook my corner of Little Italy to its foundations.

Domenico Annunziato Bellacqua was an unassuming man on all counts save one: he loved his wife, Maddalena, desperately. One day in 1977, when she was discovered in the woods of Rhode Island with another man, it did more than break Dom's heart. It threatened his identity. His tender devotion to his wife—the one high note in an otherwise drab routine of factory work and family obligation—allowed him, an unassuming man living in a strange country, to negotiate his relationships with his guardian angels, the brothers who had brought their *picculu Domenicu*, "little Dominic," to the

United States from Calabria. With his blunt fingers and bear-cub haunches, Dom's membership in this male species was never in doubt. But he lacked its dominant gene. The other Bellacqua bears sniffed out conflict as if it were leftover food at a campground. When one of them, Gianciotto, insulted my father over cards, they didn't speak for years. During the silence, my father smeared the face of every photograph of Gianciotto in our house with black Magic Marker and forbade us to utter his name. A stranger to such fits of passion, Dom was content to slog along with his factory work, raise his four pretty daughters (including the sultry Luisella), savor the black hair and white skin of his wife, and ingest the steaming bowls of *pasta al ragù* that our families often shared together, even in high summer, in one of the infinite finished basements of Little Italy.

Dom's chocolate eyes welled with the sadness of the ages. One of the youngest children in a family of nine, he enjoyed neither the domestic power that my patriarchal father wielded so decisively and often cruelly, nor the more sensual pursuits favored by Dom's older brothers: alcohol, gambling, and, for the silver-haired rake Fabrizio, *i fimmine 'mericane*, those mysterious and morally inscrutable creatures, American Women. The land of the Bellacqua brothers, the Calabrian hill town of Acri, was until recently a place that time had forgotten. Although heavy industry and the latest Western business practices filtered into the area after World War II, only in the past few decades—after the emigration of *la famiglia Bellacqua*—did Dom and my parents' region begin to overcome the devastation wrought by centuries of political corruption and Mafia control. Dom never knew this new and improved Calabria. Century in and out, daily life in his village remained unchanged. The husband earned his family's keep while the wife kept the home in order. The sons worked alongside their father until they were old enough to find a trade and procreate; then they would resume the generational cycle in another part of the village. Meanwhile, the black-haired daughters of Calabria helped their mothers with the chores, primped their hair before the bedroom mirror, and guarded that forbidden raven treasure until marriage, when they could walk across the honeymoon threshold wearing white.

When Dom and his brothers left Calabria, they smuggled their ancient worldview, *la miseria*, past U.S. customs. They sought to fashion their immigrant nation after their own image, and held on to their prejudices as tenaciously as they did their accents. *"Chisti cazzi d'americani"* ("These goddamn Americans") was my father's pet prelude to some larger point that would reveal his disdain for a culture he was forced to inhabit, but his deepest convictions prevented him from ever accepting it. It would take Maddalena's tryst to test whether the Calabrian philosophy of my father and the Bellacqua boys would survive on foreign soil. When Dom asked himself how much he loved his guilty-as-charged wife, he was also gauging whether *la miseria*, which sprang from poverty, superstition, and tradition, could exist in a prosperous, rationalist, and (to the communal mind of the Bellacquas) godless New World.

After her brother discovered Maddalena and her lover in the woods and beat her on the spot, my father assumed his duties as a leading member of our Calabrian community, convening a Council of Bellacqua Brothers to decide her fate. I was around ten at the time and have two distinct memories of the event. The first is of the barrel-chested Bellacqua men, resplendent in their leather skin and short sleeves, sitting around our upstairs table and debating with chilling calm. Here was where my father would screen any prospective suitors of my three older sisters; where we slept in rooms free from any "American" detritus (posters, decorations, and other expressions of personality); and where, every few years or so, my parents would procreate (my mom's pregnancies stretched from her sixteenth to her thirty-ninth year—a fact that always amazed me, given that she had stopped "sleeping" in my dad's room in her early thirties because of his snoring).

My second image is of Dom himself. Unlike his brothers— who would hoist me up, sing to me, or tell me (with a wince) how little I resembled my father, whom they revered—the more awkward Dom would flash me a half smile and drop his head back toward the pasta. On the day of the council, he looked dazed. I pictured Dom's head bobbing *yes, yes, yes* to one punitive measure after another, but his brown eyes spoke otherwise. No vindication sparked in them. Just the moist glow of that signature chocolate melancholy now softened even further. Though only a child, I sensed something that neither my father nor Dom's brothers knew: perhaps Dom was going to divorce them and not Maddalena. After all, they'd had it coming for centuries.

Dom belonged to an in-between generation for whom questions about ethnic identity were words from another planet. His thoughts centered on the tasks at hand: the mortgage, his overtime pay, this season's potatoes, last year's wine, and now the crime and punishment of his wife. But he seemed to understand the stakes of his upcoming decision. He felt bound, on the one hand, by the protocols and traditions of a southern Italy that he had abandoned and, on the other, by the unintelligible codes and morals of the New World, whose clothes he didn't wear, whose standards he didn't satisfy, but whose messages—whose *freedom*—he could smell in the salty ocean air of Rhode Island. His choice was stark and simple: Would he be the Calabrian moral dinosaur, staving off extinction for another generation by deferring to the dictates of his bloodline and birthplace? Or would he embrace this great new country and its easy, ad hoc principles in affairs of the heart? Would he close ranks with his brothers, the tyrannosauruses, or surrender to evolution?

The patriot Giuseppe Mazzini, a major figure in the drive for Italian unification, described the Italian family as the "country of the heart." In his typically prophetic voice, Mazzini wrote, "There is an angel in the Family who, by the mysterious influence of grace, of sweetness, and of love, renders the fulfillment of duties less wearisome, sorrows less bitter. The only pure joys unmixed with sadness which it is given to man to taste upon earth are, thanks to this angel, the joys of the Family." Had this been said of any other country, it would make us cringe—but not of Italy, where they've kept the household gods locked in the kitchen cupboard for centuries.

In the popular 1988 film *Cinema Paradiso*, the protagonist, Totò, now a famous director, returns after a twenty-year hiatus to the Sicilian island where he had grown up and worked as a projectionist. His mother and sister have aged; his room has not. His mother has kept it just as he left it, filled with his hanging bicycle and cherished movie photos. Totò had pledged to stay away when his mentor, the blind projectionist Alfredo, forbade him to return to their *paese*. His mother asks him if he wants to rest after his trip. No, he says, the flight from Rome took only an hour. You shouldn't have told me that, she replies.

Italians practice a different kind of preservation with the bedrooms of their daughters. In the most influential novel in Italian history, Alessandro Manzoni's *The Betrothed*, much of the narrative centers on the Nun of Monza. Born into an aristocratic Milanese family, she is destined from an early age for the cloisters, as her parents have focused all their efforts on preserving the family's estate for the firstborn son. To that end, they practice an unusual form of psychological torment on their daughter by pretending that, of all the lives one might choose, a nun's is finest:

> When [the Nun of Monza] was born, her father the prince wanted to give her a name which would carry immediate suggestion of the cloistered life, and which had been borne by a saint of noble birth; so he called her Gertrude [after a famous medieval mystic]. Dolls dressed as nuns were the first toys that she received; then she was given little images of female saints, always nuns again. These presents were always accompanied by urgent instructions to look after them well, as precious possessions, and by the affirmative question: "Pretty, aren't they?"

However extravagant, these words suggest what anyone who has spent time in Italy—and anyone who has grown up in an Italian family—knows: boys and girls are considered separate species. When my father convened the Council of Brothers, I had no understanding of the word *gender*. Even then, however, I sensed that the matter symbolized the battle between the Italian sexes. Did Dom think of his actions in relation to expectations about men and women, the roles they play and the identities they assume? I don't rule this out. After all, what made my father and the Bellacqua brothers act the way they did, manly men swaggering past their less macho American brethren, if not their own peculiar idea of what defined the male animal?

The flip side of the Bellacqua strut was the coddling given to Calabrian saplings, myself included. My mother, like all the women from her village, doted on her two boys. I didn't find it strange that she washed my hair over the kitchen sink all the way through high school, or that it was unusual to live in a house with floors clean enough to eat on. My mother bleached, folded, and ironed my clothes; packed my lunches; combed my hair; and (I'm mortified to admit) cleaned the wax out of my ears. It took years of my being reminded otherwise—especially and emphatically by the women in my adult life—to see that these attentions were neither normal nor healthy. It was only the advent of college, and my move away from home, that allowed me to recalibrate my distorted sense of maleness.

I wasn't the only one to struggle out of the southern Italian womb. I recently called my mother, who told me that my older brother, Angelo, who is in his sixties, had just stopped by for his weekly plate of pasta. My brother moved away from home as a teenager to go to college in Texas. He earned his tuition money by working third shift during high school and then ran in exclusive circles at Southern Methodist University, where his roommate was a nationally ranked tennis player and the son of an executive at Du Pont. His undergraduate years in Dallas involved a little study and a lot of poker. In short, he was on the fast track for southwestern success, buoyed by rich friends with all the right connections. But then he came back to Rhode Island. Back to sleepy Westerly, our family, and the usual roles. Twenty years later, he and my mom reinforce their covenant with each bowl of pasta.

My brother and I were playing our part in an ancient Italian tragicomedy.

"You can find them everywhere, handsome, charming, well-dressed men equipped with the latest cell phones and sleekest motorbikes." At first Lesley Stahl's introduction to "*Mammoni*," "Mama's Boys," in a 2001 episode of *60 Minutes* sounded like an ad for Italy's stereotypical Casanovas, Romeos, and Latin lovers. But the men featured, Davide Lucchini (age thirty-one), Massimo Malerba (forty-five), and Giorgio Boemo (thirty-nine), all shared a trait not usually associated with cutting-edge cool: they still lived at home with *mamma*. Unlike most American men in such domestic arrangements, all three of these *mammoni* were good-looking, were well turned out, and earned a solid living. Two actually owned their own houses, one of which (Giorgio's) had ocean views, state-of-the-art audio, and the latest in kitchen design.

Much as Athenian democracy was built on the sweat of the city-state's enormous slave population, the perks of *mammone* life depend on the uncomplaining industry of mothers. Giorgio's seventy-seven-year-old mom started her day at five a.m. to squeeze fresh orange juice; by seven o'clock she was on her way to church to light candles; then she went home for cooking, cleaning, and ironing. Come noontime, she prepared a presidential luncheon for Giorgio and his dad.

In another scene, a white-haired mother shipped a bag of clean laundry on the local bus for drop-off at the house of her son, who had finally flown the nest and moved across town. In Italy, unmarried men don't cut the umbilical cord and apron strings; they stretch them out. According to the London *Daily Telegraph* in 2007, 43 percent of the Italian males who finally did move out lived less than a mile from their parents—and many sent laundry home to *mamma*. This same newspaper reported that in 2011, 48 percent of young Italians between the ages of eighteen and thirty-nine lived with their parents.

Things became so bad that the Italian government established what must have been one of the most unpopular finance initiatives of all time: a tax break to lure Italian men away from home. According to *Der Spiegel*, in 2007 the parliamentarian Tommaso Padoa-Schioppa pledged 1,000 euros (about $1,300) to "send those we call *bamboccioni* ('big babies') out of the house." All sides of the political spectrum attacked him. Many taxpayers were furious that these big babies, who were already receiving free cooking, cleaning, and other household services from their unpaid mothers, would get additional booty from the state. But others countered that the situation was not the fault of the *bamboccioni*. The Communist deputy Francesco Caruso said, "Padoa-Schioppa's absurd gaffe shows how he's probably not clear how precarious is the situation afflicting an entire generation." The problem Caruso referred to was the lack of economic opportunity that has been plaguing Italy's youth for generations, which the global financial crisis of 2008 only worsened.

I experienced this lack of hope firsthand when I attended a seminar at the Italian Institute for Philosophical Studies in 1996 in Calabria. I was the only American in a group of about twenty-five students, most of whom already had their Italian undergraduate degree, the *laurea*, a specialized course of study in one subject. A few were already working as high school teachers or in some other form of secondary education. Most, however, were either unemployed or snooping around for a short-term teaching assignment or a graduate program—in America, not Italy. It astonished me that most of the new students in U.S. graduate programs in Italian were Italian rather than American. I could not imagine American students going to Italy to study American history, culture, and literature, but that was the case for Italians seeking the coveted Ph.D. This trend was doubly strange when you consider that a U.S. doctorate is no ticket to entry for the Italian university system, whose faculty is almost exclusively Italian educated. But my fellow students in the seminar assured me that they had little chance of finding work in Italian universities run by the so-called *baroni*, "barons," who distribute favors to their protégés and keep the Italian academy impervious to change. I have not kept up with my fellow seminar students, but I would wager that as a tenured college professor, I enjoy professional security they can only dream of.

Italy has long been accused of putting family first, which of course *mammoni* do by choosing to remain physically as well as emotionally ensconced within their childhood walls. In *The Moral Basis of a Backward Society* (1958), Edward Banfield studied the southern Italian town of Chiaromonte and concluded that the inhabitants were "amoral familists" who refused to "further the interest of the group or community except as it is to [their] private advantage to do so." As a result, the town lacked "civic improvement associations, organized charities, and leading citizens who take initiative in public service." Joseph LaPalombara echoed Banfield's view, arguing that for most young Italians, the family was the form of primary socialization, and that the nation's schools and other public institutions failed to provide a coherent view of the national political system. In a similar vein, Robert Putnam's landmark study *Making Democracy Work* (1993) demonstrated that the family's strong presence in southern Italian life prevented it from creating the informal civic traditions that have long defined American politics.

While Italian men enjoy a world of perks, the same cannot be said for their female counterparts, especially during the Berlusconi era. Over and above the many allegations of Berlusconi's sexual misconduct, his attitude toward women riled Italians of all political allegiances. He urged foreign businesses to invest in Italy because it had so many "beautiful secretaries." Another time, he credited his "playboy" powers with persuading Finland's female prime minister to grant Italy a key European Union agency. In 2008 Berlusconi arrived in Germany for a NATO summit hosted by Chancellor Angela Merkel, arguably the most powerful woman in the world, who stood prepared to greet him as he emerged from his motorcade—but Silvio wasn't ready. He was taking a phone call. At first Merkel smiled in understanding, but as the call went on, disbelief spread over her face before dissolving into disgust. Berlusconi remained on the phone for a full fifteen minutes.

The BBC reported in 2008 that Italy had the lowest rate

of female employment in the European Union: just 46 percent of Italian women had jobs, and the figure was much lower in the patriarchal south. Only one in five government ministers and members of Parliament is female, and women parliamentarians have included the porn star Cicciolina (who made hard-core films while in office) and the ex-stripper-showgirl Mara Carfagna, who was named one of the world's "hottest politicians" by (you guessed it) *Maxim*. Even in academia—a domain with a significant proportion of women—females are only half as likely as males to gain tenure. In 2010 the World Economic Forum ranked Italy seventy-fourth in women's rights, behind Colombia, Peru, and Romania. Most tellingly of all, Italian women spend twenty-one hours a week on housework, while Italian men spend four. Only one in twenty Italian men has ever used a washing machine.

During his two decades in power, Berlusconi used his media control to disseminate hypersexualized images of women, especially his *veline*, the scantily clad female presenters to his many variety shows. Even before his political rise, in the 1970s he offered Italians a TV quiz show in which housewives stripped off an item of clothing piecemeal, from apron to garter belt, each time a male contestant responded correctly. I had long known of such outrages, but it was only recently that the degraded state of Italian women hit home with me—by entering my living room. To understand contemporary Italy better, I subscribed to RAI Internazionale, the state-sponsored television channel that makes a selection of programming available to American viewers. Despite the notoriety of Italian television, I expected to enjoy the news and other shows about Italy today. But the vapid programming, with its *veline* and garish variety shows, ponderous historical series, and droning newscasts, soon reminded me of the stark divide between the Italy that I taught—its art, culture, and political struggles—and the plastic nation on-screen.

I might have just forgotten the RAI, along with the hundreds of other unwatched channels, were it not for some recent channel surfing. It was Saturday, the day of the Serie A soccer games, Italy's premier league in its number one sport, and I tuned in to a show introduced by a blond woman with inflated lips and exaggerated curves. She wore a sour expression, as if aware that a lecherous world was trying to stare down her neckline, and led a conversation among sportswriters sparring in front of a studio audience in a game-show atmosphere that sexualized, of all things, soccer. I am not politically correct, but I do have my limits—and a young daughter. I called my cable company and canceled my subscription.

These long, blond creatures differed from the Italian females I grew up with—when, more often than not, I was surrounded by stocky women wearing black. My matronly aunts and other relatives, some almost as wide as they were tall, always appeared to be on the wrong side of fate. Premature cancer, inexplicable accidents, and the long-term illnesses of their husbands divided them from their men with seemingly greater frequency than their taller, thinner, and lighter-haired American counterparts. Their reaction was always the same. I knew that many of the deceased had been indifferent if not violent husbands, workaholic or alcoholic, who were incapable of conversation beyond a few grunts. Yet when my mother encountered one of these newly widowed Calabrians at JCPenney, T.J.Maxx, or some christening or First Communion and offered her condolences, the crestfallen woman would fight back tears and murmur, *"Dio ha voluto così"* ("God wanted it this way"), or *"Eh, cuma', che possiamo far?"* ("Oh, friend, what can we do?").

Once, in Calabria, a distant relative invited me over for a local specialty: fusilli with roasted red peppers cooked over a kettle. She made the pasta from scratch with flour, water, and eggs and then rolled the dough into individual strands with a thin metal rod. As laborious and time-consuming as it sounds, that was the easy part. To peel the peppers, this good woman had to sit alongside her daughter for six hours and manually separate the soft inside of the red vegetable from its skin. I had never felt so humbled by someone's hospitality— and from a person I'd never met before. She was in her fifties and had the nimble step of the industrious southern Italian homemaker. Like many members of her community, she wore black. I assumed it was because her husband had died. But then in the house I saw an impromptu shrine that consisted mostly of photographs of her son, who had died in a motorbike accident as a boy more than a decade earlier. Still in mourning, she had devoted what remained of her life to her son's death. Of all the Italian women swathed in black, she was the high priestess.

From the time I was in high school, I understood that for me as for most of my peer group, life would be about choices: what college I would go to, what I would study, what career I would embark on, whom I would marry, and so forth. In my parents' Calabria, it was not what one chose, but what one was offered. Most of the women in my mother's village knew that they would be housewives and nothing else, and most of them entered into marriage with someone their families had selected for them. They did not date, did not ask themselves if what they were experiencing was true love. Unless they deviated from their expected path or found themselves widows at a young age, most of them shared their bed with one person for their entire lifetime. When that person died, whether he had been a prince or a prick, their lives as women, as sexual beings, ended. Not that they couldn't remarry, for if the woman was young enough, there was no stigma attached to starting a new family. But because most of these widows had never dated or been with any-one except for their husband, they didn't circulate in the usual sexual way. They had always understood their body as belonging to a single person. When he died, the inti-macy of man and woman died with them. This is why the widows my mother comforted shed so many tears. It was not only their husbands they were mourning; it was the young women inside them. With their thick ankles and swollen eyes, they wept over a lost connection to female pleasures and a male body that, however imperfect, had been theirs alone.

I never thought of my parents as having had a private life, let alone an intimate one. But the facts suggest otherwise: My mother met and married my father at age fourteen; she was pregnant seven times and bore six children (her first miscar-ried). He was the only man she ever knew, and their rela-tionship occupied—like an invading army—her life for half a century. For Yolanda Luzzi, her man was not merely her partner; he was a part of her. She could never conceive that so absolute a relationship allowed for substitution. *"Pasquà, guarda, guarda i criaturri che avimo fatto 'nzemi!"* ("Look, look at the children we made together!"), she cried to his body the day of his funeral. She couldn't leave her husband any more than she could leave herself.

Looking back on the Council of Brothers, it wasn't Dom's or his brothers' actions that shocked me the most. It was Maddalena's. What compelled her to break with ancient restraints and follow her desire all the way into fulfillment's desolate attic? Love? Or, more impressively original, lust? Did she sense that behind those sad eyes and inside those massive haunches Dom felt things differently from his bearish brothers? That he too, like my mother and her mournful Calabrian lady friends, was the kind of person who stood by his body-and-soul mate no matter what? If there was any terrible beauty in that event, it was this: in a Calabrian culture that left no room for surprises, especially on the gender front, the protagonists Domenico and Maddalena Bellacqua defied all expectations by following their hearts into very dangerous waters.

About a century after the birth of Italy in 1861, Dom left his figurative Naples, the provincial Calabrian capital Cosenza, to join his brothers in the United States. He brought along his daughters and wife, Maddalena. Eventually Maddalena's even more attractive younger cousin Cinzia came to the United States for an arranged marriage to an Italian American in our town. She too was discovered with another man one day—a fellow factory worker. The women in Maddalena's family, the saying goes, are cursed with beauty.

That day of the council, when the Bellacqua brothers emptied glass after glass of my father's homemade wine and plotted for the restitution of their tarnished honor, Dom didn't show the slightest interest in the state of the Italian family and its gender relations. For him, the choices were simple and stark: punish Maddalena as ordered and, in so doing, perpetuate in a strange land the familiar patterns of justice and retribution that had sustained his people for centuries; or turn his back on his brothers and *la miseria* by following his aching heart all the way back to the arms of his scarlet-lettered wife. Though the prospect of doing something "American" was the last thing on Dom's mind, his journey from Acri, Calabria, to Westerly, Rhode Island, was a restaging of the American Dream. Dom couldn't have heard a slogan as naive as "Go West!" when he was deciding about Maddalena, because when southern Italians traveled to the New World, they thought more about what they were leaving than where they were heading. Dom's first journey west in the early 1970s, from Calabria to Rhode Island, turned out to be just the first stage of an even longer road away from *la miseria* and toward the setting sun: Domenico Bellacqua, one of the last people on earth you would imagine on the shores of the Pacific, eventually settled in California.

A decade ago I attended a conference in San Francisco, and before I set out, my family suggested that I look up Dom. As I walked along the city's waterfront, there seemed no more incongruous place for him to wind up. Its deep, dull blue sky, pastel stucco buildings, and long, athletic bodies promised cheerful oblivion to any traveler who made the place home. Who could bother with matters like the Southern Question in sixty-degree sunshine in late December? The miserable New York winter I had left behind seemed as remote to me as that day in 1977 when the inherited centuries of honor codes, male hierarchies, and folk wisdom all conspired to seal the fate of Dom's wife.

Or so you would have guessed. In fact, Dom rejected his brothers' final judgment—that he disown Maddalena immediately and forever—and took his wife back, forgiving her completely. The stunning reversal disgraced him in the eyes of our Little Italy. My dad continued to speak to Dom and act hospitably toward him. After the requisite term of exile, he even allowed Maddalena back into our house. But to himself and his friends (and especially the Bellacqua brothers), my father's position was clear: Dom had shamed himself and his family by allowing *"chija puttana,"* "that whore," to betray him and his family without suffering reprisal. The English translation for Dom's untouchable caste as *cornuto*, the Shakespearean-sounding "cuckold," fails to register what my father and the Bellacqua brothers understood to be the main cause for Dom's unmanning. He had lost the one thing that *la miseria* could take from no man—no matter how dangerous the Mafia threat, barren the harvest, or vicious the northern racism: his sexual honor. Dom had stared into the ancient, unblinking eyes of the Southern Question only to give up the world for love. His Californian exile had translated into a classic American tale: his childrens' successful business; the rapidly appreciating real estate (we're talking northern California in the 1980s and '90s); the steady thickening of frame; the gradual erosion of health through easy living. I never did contact him.

In 2011 Dom died of cancer. By this time, there were few dealings between his family and mine. When he was last on the East Coast a few years earlier, he stayed with his sister

Mariuccia, who had supported him throughout his and Maddalena's ordeal without passing judgment. Dom refused to visit my widowed mother during his trip, a ceremonial snub that she reciprocated by refusing to invite him to our home. During his time back east, Dom and my mother did see each other at a procession for Our Lady of Mount Carmel, a religious celebration in honor of the Virgin Mary. They said hello, kissed on the cheeks, and exchanged looks as cold as the surface of the moon. Dom and Maddalena remained happily married until he succumbed, and Maddalena has apparently put on her share of cheerful pink pounds after moving west. They say that her white skin has barely aged.

A lot has changed in the way Italian Americans relate to their southern Italian origins since Maddalena's affair in 1977, just as the roles of men and women in Italy now differ from what they were three decades ago. But one thing Dom did remains timeless. In taking the hard, high road and treating his wife with compassion even as she humiliated him, he showed a largeness of spirit that I had never seen before. My idea of a hero back then involved the ability to throw a baseball or tackle someone hard enough to hurt him. But my limited moral self could sense that Dom had done something unusual, even extraordinary. If I close my eyes now and think back to that Council of Brothers, with their leather skin and cast-iron potbellies, I understand how much courage it took for Dom to stand up to his Pleistocene brethren. Rather than add to their brick wall of judgment against his beloved, betraying wife, he chose to walk around it, not knowing if anyone—especially Maddalena—would be waiting on the other side.

4

The Fig Tree and the Impala

My father pronounced the number six "sex." With his firm jaw and wavy salt-and-pepper hair, he cut a *bella figura*. So the gas station attendant never smirked when he asked for "sex unleaded"—and, I imagine, the checkout girl would blush when she placed his "sex bananas" on the scale. I had a back-row seat to all this. By the time I was born, my father was already in his forties and had four other, grown children to worry about. Plus, I was a boy. It was *i fimmine*, "the ladies," who ate up his show.

My family's heroic age—military uniforms, toothless ancestors, roasted chestnuts—was the stuff of black-and-white photographs that my mom kept in a bedside drawer. Though the suburbs of Rhode Island provided everything Italy had denied my siblings, including Little League, a liberal arts education, and a sense of entitlement, my brother and sisters had something I lacked: a history spanning Caesar's conquest of Gaul, Michelangelo's chisel, and Galileo's telescope. My senior essay on Ben Johnson's Roman tragedies and a Eurail excursion through Lombardy just didn't compete. Nowhere does that history loom larger than in a

My father and
his children in
Calabria, shortly
before their
passage to the
United States

family photograph from 1956. My father is dressed in his
only suit, flanked by his four children. Framed by the burnt
hills of Calabria, he is poised to shepherd his children out of
their village and through immigration. His wife, their mother,
awaits in *l'America*, their new home.

This first family shared more than hopes and fears: they
spoke the same dialect. My parents never had to remind me
that the Calabrian of my siblings was off-limits. I understood
this by watching my brother and sisters shed it like dead skin
each day. But I never imagined they could be as American as
I was, any more than I could be a real Italian like them. My
parents had neither America nor Italy, only each other. Too
set in their ways and their language to remake themselves,
they chose instead to live as if they were still in the Old Coun-

try. Hence the goat, the winepress, and the hand-laid stone walls. A couple as inseparable as they were couldn't help but fight so much: the geography of their lives shrank to a few suburban acres and the imagined trajectories of their children.

For my parents, the rush to make mortgage payments and find extra money for the birthday of a godchild or the wedding of a cousin didn't take place in the shadow of that history I coveted. My brother and sisters, for their part, were too attuned to the malls, fast food, and secretarial pools of their surroundings for Calabrian lore to have remained central to their lives. Soon enough, no one in my family but my parents could speak the dialect.

Some thirty years after that photograph in the Calabrian hills was taken, my parents traveled to Italy to settle my grandmother Rosaria's estate. Before leaving, they made no mention of the sites they would visit in Rome. They discussed only the old friends they would look up and the distant relatives they hoped were still alive. I had expected them to return to Italy as tourists. After all, they were no longer Italian citizens, and nearly everyone close to them had immigrated to the United States as well. But for my parents Calabria had long since ceased to be a living region. The land where my grandmother died was the same place where my mother and father had buried their former lives. Their return to Calabria was no homecoming; it was a haunting. Worst of all, they still spoke the same language as those too-familiar ghosts.

Two decades after my parents' return to Calabria, I took the morning train from Florence to Milan to visit the museum dedicated to Italy's most famous novelist, Alessandro Manzoni. His stately town house in central Milan stood in a courtyard bordered on one side by the family garden and on the other by a bank that now owns it. The celebrated La Scala opera house lies a few blocks away, and the Gothic Duomo and arches of the Victor Emmanuel II shopping gallery are also within walking distance.

A heavy, bemused security guard led me to a sunken study in the ground floor of the museum. Here, Manzoni had spent much of his life writing, revising, and translating his monumental novel, *I promessi sposi* (*The Betrothed*), the story of two peasant fiancés, Renzo Tramaglino and Lucia Mondella, who are unable to marry because the evil nobleman Don Rodrigo pursues the incorruptible Lucia and casts into exile the hapless, hotheaded Renzo. The novel's events unfold against a backdrop of plague and Spanish domination in seventeenth-century Lombardy. One critic called *The Betrothed* the allegory for all of Italian history: "While Manzoni's immediate story is simply a concrete episode taken from Italian popular life—the love, separation, and reunion of a young peasant boy and girl—his presentation transforms it into a general tragedy of the Italian people." For all its brilliant themes, the novel's greatest gift to Italy was its language. Manzoni's first, unpublished version of the book, completed in 1823 with the unfortunate title *Fermo and Lucia* (the original names of the peasant protagonists), was a linguistic catchall that included elements from his native Lombard as well as a random sprinkling of other northern dialects. There was no "Italian" to write in then: Italy wouldn't be unified until 1861. Manzoni believed that the birth of Italy depended on its ability to create a single language from the peninsula's various dialects. So he spent years in a task as dreary as it was necessary: translating *The Betrothed* into the Tuscan of Dante, Petrarch, and Boccaccio, the dialect that he helped make the language of his united country.

I stood beside the desk where the slight but distinguished-looking Manzoni had bent over thousands of pages in the novel's three versions (1823, 1827, and 1840). Meanwhile, the guard detailed Alessandro's typical day. Hours of reading and writing in the morning; a walk in the garden or a chat with his friend, the notary and novelist Tommaso Grossi, who worked in an adjacent study; then time upstairs in the afternoon with his ever-growing family (he sired nine children in two marriages). Manzoni suffered from nausea and shortness of breath when he left his house or encountered crowds. I used to find it ironic that so civic-minded a writer found human contact unbearable. But his agoraphobia began to make sense as I stood beside the wood-and-leather desk, surrounded by cracked volumes on philosophy, politics, and natural history, all locked behind glass in high-backed shelves. The only traces of Manzoni's personality were the scars and scratches on his desk.

Not long after the final edition of *The Betrothed*, Manzoni wrote a strange book entitled *On the Historical Novel*, which announced that his masterpiece had been ill conceived. *The Betrothed*, he wrote, was not properly "historical," because it contained material invented by the author's imagination. Nor was it truly a "novel," because so many of its details derived from the public record. He vowed to stop writing fiction altogether in order to dedicate himself to the more sober tasks of the historian. This was Manzoni's

Portrait of Alessandro
Manzoni by Francesco
Hayez (1841)

stated word, in any case. I believe he bade farewell to the
novel that brought him renown because he thought that
Italy could no longer afford the luxury of make-believe during its drive for unification. The same patriotic spirit that compelled him to spend thirteen years translating *The Betrothed*
into Tuscan may also have conspired to divorce him from art.
The same desk that had absorbed his spirit in the name of the
Italian language then did so in the name of Italian unity.

I had entered not just the library of Italy's most important modern writer but the heart of the Italian language—
one as removed from my parents' Calabrian as Manzoni's
town house was from the hut where my parents raised their
Italian-born children.

•

The language problem in Italy is so momentous that it has its
own name: the *questione della lingua*. The land initially founded
as seven hills in Rome in 753 B.C. remained, in the words of
the Austrian statesman Metternich, "a mere geographical expression" for centuries, during which time each region or city
spoke a dialect of its own. For Dante, the new language of
Italy still needed to be invented. According to his aristocratic idea, this unifying tongue was to be the "illustrious
vernacular," an amalgam of the best elements from each Italian dialect. What is striking is the license Dante grants to
poets, the guardians of language, to shape Italy's linguistic
future. He exhorts his fellow authors to preserve the dignity
of everyday speech and shun vulgar expression. His rules are
rigid. Words in harmony with their Latin roots (say, the Italian *amore* from the Latin *amor*) are acceptable, whereas harsh-
sounding words—for example, the Sienese *chesto* for *questo*,
"this"—are not. But by the end of Dante's life, the illustrious vernacular remained like Italy itself: an unattainable
abstraction.

Dante's great service to Italian unification was not his
language treatise, but his fourteen-thousand-line poem, *The
Divine Comedy* (c. 1305–21). It would have been natural for
him to write this epic in the language of the learned, Latin.
But Dante, whose *Eloquence in the Vernacular* aimed to show
that the dialects of Italy had a worthy history in their own
regard, could never accept the limitations in expression that
a dead language like Latin would pose. In 1827, Manzoni
made a pilgrimage to Dante's Florence and famously pro-
claimed that he wanted to *"risciacquare i panni"* ("rinse the

laundry") in the city's Arno River, the symbol of Tuscan's preeminence as a literary language. Florence became an ideal cultural homeland for Manzoni just as it was for its native son Dante, who I believe wrote his *Comedy* in Tuscan partly because he wished to inhabit the words of the city that had exiled him. Toward the end of Dante's life, a renowned scholar invited him to become poet laureate of Bologna, but he declined. Only Florence, Dante said, could extend this invitation—only in the shadows of the Baptistery, his baptismal font, would he accept the laurel crown.

After Dante, the Tuscan dialect continued to flourish in exile. Petrarch composed his elegies to Laura—written in France—in Tuscan because his family, like Dante's, had been banished from Tuscany for political reasons. About the time of the French Revolution, the Turinese Vittorio Alfieri moved to Florence to write his heroic plays and rid his work of French influences (in his words, to "Tuscanize" and "de-Frenchify" himself). Manzoni, too, would exile himself from his native Lombard and translate *The Betrothed* into Tuscan, the future language of Italy and Manzoni's most lasting contribution to the Risorgimento, the movement that led to unification.

And so a historical accident—that such gifted authors as Dante, Petrarch, and Boccaccio composed in Tuscan seven hundred years ago—helped create the language now spoken in the Italian senate, in outdoor markets from the Alps to the Aeolian Islands, and in Italian 101 classrooms throughout the world. But making Tuscan the official voice of the nation did not dampen the sound of Italy's many dialects. Though the educated and prosperous had access to the linguistic unity brought about by the efforts of the likes of Dante and Manzoni, Italy's illiterate and poor still spoke a Babel of local idioms, syntaxes, and mutually incomprehensible accents. Only the diffusion of Tuscan Italian through such democratic means as television and compulsory education would lead the country to a more universal language.

Italy's language, like its culture, is easy to love but difficult to understand. For example, everyone assumes that words ending in *a*, as in *bella donna*, "beautiful woman," are feminine. But many cognates that end in *a* are masculine, including the Greek-derived *programma*, "program"; *sistema*, "system"; and *tema*, "theme." There's even more of a challenge in the spelling, a term rarely used in Italian because it's a phonetic language where words are spelled as spoken. As a result, in Italian you must pronounce each letter and syllable or risk embarrassment: *sette* means "seven," but *sete* means "thirst"; *anno* means "year," but *ano* means "anus." The dependence of Italian on clear and accurate pronunciation makes it a theatrical language, something spoken and sung in equal measure.

Subtlety and delicacy, not good old American directness, carry the day in professional dealings in Italy. So it is with written language. In American English, we prize concision and clarity. But if an Italian were to write in this manner, he would be judged to lack style and verbal flair. The love of rhetoric defines Italian society, whether you're in an open market haggling down the price of fresh fish or in front of your professor taking an oral exam. In the Italian language, it's better to be beautiful than to be good. The heirs of Dante do not hand in a *grande*, "great," or *buono*, "good," exam, but rather a *bello*, "beautiful," one. One is just as likely to have a *bell'idea* as a *buon'idea*. And when a scandal is particularly juicy, it's *un bello scandolo*. Most important of all, when you do something nice for someone, or when you act with grace or savoir faire, you are presenting a *bella figura*, which combines kindness and civility with a not-so-selfless desire to be acknowledged. If it were just a "good" or *"buona" figura*, then nobody would have had to witness the gesture; its beauty derives from the spectacle.

As you might expect in a country known for its equivocations (Italy changed sides in both world wars), the subjunctive mood dominates. In English, most verbs are in the indicative mood, in that they indicate, declare, or advertise something. Though we use the subjunctive in English (If it *were* up to me . . .), the Italians have by comparison a much moodier language. Their ubiquitous subjunctive expresses doubt, worry, fear, hope, or something unique or exceptional. The most famous subjunctive in Italian belongs to Dante. In *Inferno* 26, Dante meets the most notorious politician of the preceding generation, the formidable *volpe*, "fox," Guido da Montefeltro, who greets the Pilgrim with a winding triple subjunctive:

> *S'i' credesse che mia risposta fosse*
> *a persona che mai tornasse al mondo,*
> *questa fiamma staria sanza più scosse.*

> (If I but thought that my response were made
> to one perhaps returning to the world,
> this tongue of flame would cease to flicker.)

The shift from the first (*credesse*) to the second (*fosse*) and third (*tornasse*) subjunctive forms, followed by the conditional (*staria*),

reveals Guido's diabolical logic. He is a man of double en-
tendres and backroom diplomacy. His tortuous phrasing
shows why he was the most feared diplomat of his age—the
master of the contingent and hypothetical. He could be a
spokesman for the Italian language, which always registers
the half measure and the provisional. No wonder that the
ultimate poem of modern indecision, T. S. Eliot's "The Love
Song of J. Alfred Prufrock," features Guido's dizzying subjunctive as its epigraph.

The shifts and subtleties of the Italian language are all the
more complicated because, geographically speaking, there
are two Italies: a wealthier, more "European" Italy above
Rome, and a poorer and more corrupt Mezzogiorno. To this
day, a separatist movement such as the Lega Nord (Northern
League) continues to garner up to 8 percent of the national
vote by proposing to break up the country and do away with
the poverty, organized crime, and economic crises of the
south.

The generations before my father's had a response to the
poverty and suffocating traditions of the Mezzogiorno: America. This word meant not just the United States but also
the whole Western Hemisphere, from Toronto to Santiago.
Whether it meant opening up a pizzeria in Brooklyn, running numbers in Providence, or herding cattle on Las Pam-
pas, *l'America* became a password whose possessors remained
ignorant of the differences separating a Canadian from a
Brazilian. What mattered was that there were people on the
other side of the ocean who didn't know that Italy's upper
half was considered better than its lower half. Calabrians, to
be sure, also dreamed of moving to Florence or Turin for a
better way of life, and many did leave the south for such

great factories of the north as Fiat. But up north, a southerner's accent, clothes, and table manners would expose him as an outsider. In a no-place, in America, it was easier to invent yourself.

Like the immigrants who speak it, my family's southern Italian dialect masks its origins. During a summer afternoon on the beaches of Diamante or in a café in Cosenza, if you close your eyes to the sounds, you will lose your bearings. Vowels that linger without resolution might transport you to the open markets of Damascus or Riyadh or, when word endings are cut off by a swallowed consonant, perhaps to a tapas bar in Seville or a coffee stand in Caracas. Though Italian is more lyrical than Calabrian, it lacks the dialect's subtlety of mood. The Calabrian masculine definite article is *u*, as in *u libru* for *il libro*, "the book," and *u signuru* for *il signore*, "the gentleman." This exotic-sounding *u* reminds us that Calabria was a political crossroads that encompassed the influences of many foreigners, including the Arabs, Austrians, French, Greeks, and Spanish.

Most of us will never have to give up our language. We may have to refine our way of speaking or master the jargon of computer programs, legal terms, medical procedures, sales protocols, and the like. Some of us, like me, even make their living as a teacher or translator of foreign words. For my father, life abroad meant never being able to express himself in the language of the people in charge, whether they were the foremen of his airplane-parts factory or the estate owners in Weekapaug and Watch Hill, Rhode Island, where he cut lawns and planted gardens on the side. His lifelong dream was to start his own landscaping business, but he feared getting tripped up in a foreign language and alien culture. So he never left the factory and, instead of investing in a new career, buried his hard-won savings at the local credit union.

The wealthy Manzoni never had to abandon his dreams because of language. Yet the burden of self-translation into Tuscan did separate him from his native Lombard dialect. Dante continued throughout his life to write in the Florentine idiom of his birth, even after the long exile from his city at age thirty-six. But his relationship to his native speech changed as his distance, actual and spiritual, from Florence increased. During his exile he stopped writing in the Sweet New Style, the language of poetic apprenticeship that he first used to describe his love for Beatrice in the youthful autobiography, the *Vita nuova* (*New Life*, 1295). In *The Divine Comedy*, he rejected the refined erotic poetry of the Sweet New Style along with many of the poets who wrote in it, including his mentor and first best friend, the aristocratic Florentine poet Guido Cavalcanti. Dante was even implicated in Guido's death: in his capacity as one of Florence's six ruling priors in 1300, he signed the edict that exiled the political radical Guido, who died of malaria contracted abroad that same year. Though *The Divine Comedy* is written in Tuscan dialect, it consigns many of the Florentine words and figures from Dante's youth—including Cavalcanti's father—to the flames of hell.

Whatever language my father gave up, he was ultimately a man of few words. In the fall, when the leaves and shoots of the spring and summer had withered and died, he would collect them in his garden and set them on fire. These flames were the closest that my dad, a non-churchgoer—"Tell the priest I'm the dee-ble [devil]," he liked to joke to my pious brother-in-law—came to Communion. He would look into the fire in silence, no longer aware of me or anyone else. I wondered what went through his mind as he stared at the yellow, orange, and red flames, the fire crackling with a language he could communicate to nobody. It was his sole fluency, the voice of nature, and he would take it with him when he left the world. There's always a limit to how much anyone can sacrifice, even for a man like my father, whose life had been spent sustaining a large family and helping an extended network of brothers, sisters, nieces, and nephews establish themselves in America. Here, before the fire, I had my rare glimpse into that off-limits space that was his and his alone. My father may have given me life, but he never let me inside this silence.

In Milan, after spending the morning looking for signs of Manzoni in his study and town house, I was escorted out by the guard during the museum's lunch break. I decided to take some photos before eating, but the city overwhelmed me. However busy and crowded I found Florence, Milan's cobblestone tramways and boutique-filled avenues reminded me that I was looking for nineteenth-century culture amid twenty-first-century industry. The starkly tailored Milanese exuded a cool at odds with the faith and paternalism that had guided Manzoni in his twenty-year odyssey through the pages of *The Betrothed*, which ends happily thanks to God's benevolence. Renzo and Lucia marry; Don Rodrigo perishes during the bubonic plague; and the peasant couple's most fearsome obstacle, a fellow so rotten he's called the Unnamed, converts to Christianity. I pictured Manzoni at that wood-and-leather desk in his study with the growing metropolis humming outside his windows. The symmetrical shrubs of the garden and the uniform columns of his books must have formed a buffer as he ground away at his Lombard, kneading the phrases into Tuscan with the help of the Florentine governess with whom he kept up a steady correspondence that was filled with childlike questions about proverbs, semantics, and grammar.

Manzoni seemed to live forever. His eighty-eight years began in Italy's version of the French Enlightenment: his maternal grandfather was the acclaimed Italian philosopher Cesare Beccaria, author of an important treatise against the death penalty, *On Crimes and Punishments* (1764); and the man rumored to be Alessandro's natural father was a scion of Milan's leading intellectual aristocrats, the Verri. Manzoni died just a decade or so after the long-awaited unification of Italy, which honored him by naming him senator in 1860. Sitting at his desk, he envisioned an Italy that would respect Christian doctrine and surrender to God's wisdom—a nation that would speak one language culled from the pages of another literary work that also prophesied a new Italy along Christian lines, *The Divine Comedy*. Manzoni's Italy would, above all, allow unlettered peasants like Renzo and Lucia and my father access to the foreign languages of social distinction, legal code, and theological precept. That desk was no place for dreams. Page by page, Italian crisis to Italian crisis, his translation plowed ahead.

My camera ran out of batteries as I snapped the Duomo. Bouncing from one plastic bar awning to another, I began to despair of finding real food in the city center, but then someone directed me to what I was told was a decent trattoria. Inside there were many locals, but my *fettuccine al ragù* smacked of the factory, and the meal came with vacuum-packed breadsticks instead of fresh bread. The spirits ran higher at a table beside me. A group of about eight priests, all in vestments and clerical collars, luxuriated in multiple courses of antipasti, meats, cheeses, and red wine. It was not a scene I was accustomed to back home. For a fleeting moment I might have been back in the pages of Manzoni's novel, reading about the ample lunch of the cowardly parish priest Don Abbondio (who gave in to Don Rodrigo's threats and refused to marry Renzo and Lucia), or about a meal at the Half Moon Tavern, where a fugitive Renzo is arrested for stirring public unrest during the Milanese bread riots of 1628. Out of instinctual respect for the happy clerics, I tried not to listen to their conversation amid the clink of silverware and rumble of chairs. Meanwhile, the bottles of Pellegrino and flasks of wine were emptied and replenished.

Later that afternoon in the stuffy Manzoni library, I made halfhearted attempts at research under the vigilant eye of the head archivist and ended up overpaying for some photocopies. By the time I boarded the Intercity train at Milano Centrale, the only evidence of my hero's legacy was the image of the feasting priests. Manzoni's pockmarked miniature desk, the Archimedean point on which he had balanced the future of Italy, had swallowed up the rest of him.

On that train from Milan to Florence, I heard an itinerant laborer from Turkey describe his young daughter to an Italian woman. He spoke in heavy accents between asides in his native language to his gnarled father. The train hummed with other regional accents and dialects, their volume and variety on the increase as the train sped south toward Rome

and Naples. Italian may be the nation's official language, but
the dialects endure. A large population in the Alto Adige, a
northeastern territory awarded to Italy after the defeat of the
Austro-Hungarian Empire in 1918, continues to speak German, which roughly 300,000 Italians consider their mother
tongue. More than 100,000 Italians in Piedmont speak a dialect of the ancient Occitanic and Franco-Provençal, and another 50,000 in the Veneto use Slovene. The country also
contains 50,000 speakers of Ladin in the Dolomites and
30,000 Greek speakers in southern Italy. There are 15,000
speakers of Catalan in the northwest of Sardinia, and 100,000
Sicilians communicate in Arbëreshë, a dialect of Albanian.

The Italian woman told the Turkish man that his daughter was beautiful; he asked if she had children; she said no, he
said you will someday, and she said I don't think so. Though
there was little left of Manzoni in fashionable Milan, he had
done his part in enabling a well-dressed woman from northern Italy to fuss over the child of a Turkish-born textile
vendor.

My family played out its own version of the dialect drama
on that Intercity train. My siblings and I knew we spoke differently from the "Italians." We said *"allo"* upon answering
the telephone and not *"pronto,"* the way they did in Milan and
Florence. I couldn't help but see the distance between my
Little Italy and the Big Italy in Europe as a mark of cultural
inferiority, especially when I noticed my parents foundering
in the language of Dante. An occasional telephone call from
Italy would require them to speak in standard Italian. As
soon as I heard them say, *"Buon giorno, signora, La preghiamo*

di informarci . . ." ("Good morning, madame, would you kindly let us know . . ."), I felt something in my gut. The words reminded me that neither my family nor I was truly Italian. But at least we weren't "Italo-Americans," that photogenic Hollywood hybrid who, as Coppola's *Godfather* films would have us believe, could kill in the name of honor and minutes later savor fresh cannoli.

The difference between a dialect and a language, the expression goes, is that the latter of the two has an army. My family's Calabrian dialect took orders from not one but two formidable linguistic forces: the language of the Italy they had left behind and the American English they now struggled to use. Both of these idioms were foreign occupiers. At the time of unification, fewer than 10 percent of Italians used the official, Tuscan-derived Italian as their first language, and even today many still employ their dialect to express their private thoughts—jokes, confessions, declarations of love and hate. Likewise, the English grammar I studied in grade school disciplined my thoughts. But it was the tender and violent sentiments of my parents' Calabrian that taught me how to feel.

The Italian philosopher Giambattista Vico believed that the more advanced a civilization becomes, the more it loses touch with its origins—the violent yet also creative period that produces its vital forms of cultural expression. As societies progress, their language becomes abstract and cut off from the words of its robust ancestors. An early warrior would never say the bland *I'm angry*; he would wax metaphorical with *my blood boils*. With the passage of time, a poetic way of perceiving the world disappears, leaving us with what Vico calls the "barbarism of reflection."

The Roman poet Horace also believed that when words die, they take memories with them. Just as forests change their leaves each year, he writes, so too do words: "the old race dies," and like the young of humankind, new languages "bloom and thrive." "We are doomed to death—we and all things ours . . . All mortal things shall perish, much less shall the glory and glamour of speech endure and live." We can never know a people or a culture that has preceded us, he suggests, because the words they used withered and fell like the autumn leaves.

If Vico and Horace are right, then what happens when the memories of an entire people depend on languages that differ from region to region—even town to town? How can we ever understand Italian identity when there was no such thing as the Italian language until only recently? From an early age I knew I spoke "better" English and Italian than anyone else in my family. But this unloved and unwanted correctness separated me from what was most magical about my background. Surrounded by the captivating similes of literature and the stolid conjugation tables of grammar books, I knew I was no Achilles. My blood would never boil.

After a decade in America my father decided to buy a fancy car. The Italian for "a car" is *una macchina*, the Calabrian equivalent *'na macchina*. But in the car-crazy suburbs of postwar America, an immigrant such as my father was bound to defer to his host nation. He went to the Chevy dealership and asked for *'nu carru*. *Macchina* stands for anything mechanical, while *carro* is an Italian American rendition of "car." The

dialect *'nu* sounds like "new," and *carro* means "cart." So my
father, who had spent his life on farms surrounded by beasts
of burden and their modes of transportation, found himself
purchasing a "new cart"—a maroon 1967 Chevy Impala. He
bought it the year that I, his first American child, was born.

The dialect flourished in my childhood. My father's fits
of anger spawned creative verbal twists: *"mala nuova ti vo' ve-
nire"* ("may a new harm befall you"), when you annoyed
him; *"ti vo' pigliare 'na shcuppettata"* ("may you be shot") and
"ti vo' brusciare l'erba" ("may the ground beneath you catch
fire"), when you really got under his skin. It's difficult to
translate these makeshift phrases. Better to imagine them
uttered by a man who could pick up a small backyard shed.

My mother's speech was less the product of her passions,
though she faced her own Herculean linguistic challenges.
Her household duties demanded terms and appliances that
didn't exist in Calabria, so she invented an impromptu domestic lexicon. In the end, like my father and his *carru*, my
mother was prone to transliteration. There were no freezers
in her Italy, so when she wanted to preserve goods on ice,
she talked about *frizzare*, "to freeze," rather than the standard *congelare*. Other times, when her children got the best of
her, she threw her hands up and added a vowel. We did the
laundry in a *uascinga mascina*, "the washing machine," cleaned
the carpet with a *vachiuma cleena*, "the vacuum cleaner," and
drank lemonade on *u porciu*, "the porch."

My family belonged to its own ethnic group, with a private language to boot. On Sundays we crowded into the
Impala and drove along the shore past stone mansions and
rainbow-colored flower gardens just like the ones my father
weeded and watered. I imagined that behind those green

shutters and circular driveways lay America, and nothing was going to keep us from it. They drank milk with dinner behind those ivy trellises and said "mom" and "dad," while I said *"mamma"* and *"papà."* Each of those children had a room of his own, while I shared mine with a brother and, for a time, even a sister. But I referred to my father with that accented *papà.* Though only seven, I sensed the austerity of that final stressed syllable. As ashamed as I was of my parents' Italian, I couldn't have been prouder of their English. Each of them would answer calls for me by saying "she's a no' home." I took this gender-bending as an assertion of my individuality, my access to a world that separated me from all the other kids on the block. I may have lived in a three-bedroom split-level just like everyone else, but damn it, we were different. My family had no need to worship the idols of the second- and third-generation immigrants, with their cries of *"vafancul',"* *"che cazzo,"* and *"mamma mia."* When my father swore at me in Italian, he did so out of anger, not nostalgia.

This authenticity extended to the table. While my friends with grandparents from Sicily talked about Italian food, my parents produced it. Each year they churned out hundreds of jars of preserved peaches, pears, and tomatoes; gallons of red wine; and bushels of cucumbers, peas, and potatoes. Plus the showpiece crop, squash.

One year, the local paper took a photo of my father and his prizewinning, five-foot-long gourds. Sensing that he was on display, he stayed silent for the whole shoot. He didn't understand how feeding your family could translate into a human-interest story. But make no mistake: he was proud to have created such a prodigious vegetable, and he made sure the part in his hair was just so when the picture snapped. In the photo, my father's waves and curls lay flat. His face was wrinkled, and he had to lean on his cane when he reached for the prize gourd. Old age had been forced upon him prematurely by his stroke.

The day the photo was taken, my father chatted with the photographer about his legendary squash. The caption to the image was in English, and the house in the background was a nondescript 1950s model, but the fig tree and sloping plots of peas and corn evoked the hills of the Italy he had left behind. By then he had ten grandchildren, not one of whom spoke a word of Calabrian. His six children struggled to exchange greetings in dialect. The results were official: we had become Italian American, even if we still bought records featuring accordions and Calabrian folk dances, even if we still serenaded our spouses the night before marrying them.

My father struggled to explain how he grew his vegetables. He had only Calabrian words for the plants, procedures, and tools. Each of his children had attained some form of higher education and with it freedom from the strife and poverty that had chased him from Italy. They now found his background primitive and remote. He had translated or "carried over" both a family and a dialect. After all this, he believed it was his right to talk about his squash on his own terms. Around the time of the photo he poured a cement base for his picnic table. Before it dried, he signed it with a branch: "*P. L. Nato Acri 1923.*" Pasquale Luzzi, born in Acri, Italy, 1923. He died just months later, at the end of summer in 1995. In the obituary, my father's passion for gardening was listed as his "hobby," a word that didn't exist in his Calabrian.

•

After he died, I heard my father's voice, but I couldn't fill it with words. When I forced him to speak to me in English, it sounded pedantic and prissy. His Italian, though, was no less stilted, either when I tried to revive my Calabrian or when I used the textbook grammar that was unnatural to both of us. I had so much to say but no way to say it, a reflection of our relationship during his lifetime. Without his words, I lost a way of describing the world. Memories now mattered more than ever before, and I didn't know if I could find the language to keep them alive.

As the years passed, my father would surprise me, especially during family rituals. When I moved furniture, lugging chests and drawers under his imaginary surveillance, I waited for him to shout directions or criticize my work. On Christmas Eve, when I surveyed the mounds of fish on our table and decanted the homemade wine, I could hear him outside, filling up with toasts and warnings and preparing to choreograph the distribution of gifts and blessings as he stumbled down the pathway leading to the back door. After he died, we continued the annual ritual of burying the fig tree each fall and unearthing it again for planting in the spring. When I met with my family to dig this winter bed in November, my father's voice warned me not to step on the branches of his *ficuzza*. And when our neighbor, his best friend, asked me over for a drink, it was with my father's words that I answered, *"Sì, Michele, faccimuci 'nu bicchieru"* ("Yes, we'll pour a glass").

Dante wrote in his treatise on language that though men and women must communicate with words, angels can talk to one another in silence. Speaking with someone who has died is similar. You learn early on that it is best to concentrate on the person you've lost with as little verbal clutter as possible. Perhaps this Calabrian I now speak with my father is the truly dead dialect, the language that neither changes nor translates. When I think of him now, I see him digging in his garden, unearthing the *ficuzza* from its winter slumber and propping it up for the upcoming spring. But once I put a word to this picture, once this *ficuzza* becomes a *fico* or a "fig tree," he will have left me. This is when mourning becomes memory, and it's time to say goodbye to a language and a person I knew all too briefly.

PART III

A PARADISE OF EXILES

5

No Society

On November 12, 2011, a mob of Romans waving banners and chanting "Mafioso!" and "Jail! Jail! Jail!" swarmed Italy's presidential palace. Some of the demonstrators sported masks recalling Venice's Carnevale; others danced and drank champagne while singers filled the night air with Handel's "Hallelujah Chorus." In the nearby Italian Parliament, Prime Minister Silvio Berlusconi had just announced that he would step down as head of government, ending the longest rule in Italian politics since that of Mussolini. A black armored Audi was now transporting Berlusconi to a farewell meeting with the Italian president, where he would officially tender his resignation. The delirious crowd awaited.

From across the Atlantic, I watched Berlusconi skulk into his Audi and felt two eras ending, one public and the other private. The endless crises of the Berlusconi years had threatened to dissolve the nation's already fragile unity. Closer to home, the mess reminded me of why my family had fled a country that they believed offered their children no future. Unlike many Italian Americans, I harbored no romantic notions about the mother country. Yes, I loved

Italy—so deeply that I made it my career—and I clamored to explain the nation's recent turmoil to the non-Italian public. But my concern was more professional than personal as I watched the Italian government crumble that November night.

The drive from Parliament to the presidential palace covers some of the most hallowed ground in Italian history. Just west of Piazza del Parlamento stands Piazza Navona, an ancient racetrack that houses Bernini's *Fountain of the Four Rivers* and the Obelisk of Domitian, a jutting stone needle dating back to the early emperors. The route skirts the fortresslike Palazzo Venezia, where Mussolini often stood on a first-floor balcony to address feverish Roman crowds much like the one now toasting the end of the Berlusconi age.

Mussolini reviews his troops (1937)

South of Palazzo Venezia lies Via delle Botteghe Oscure, once the base of Berlusconi's and Mussolini's eternal straw men, the Communists. This street connects to Via Caetani where, on May 9, 1978, the body of the former Italian premier Aldo Moro was found riddled with the bullets of the terrorist Red Brigades. To the southeast of the presidential palace stands Trajan's Column, from A.D. 113, on the Forum of Julius Caesar opposite the Colosseum. Human memory, Freud wrote, was like Rome: an endless layering of periods and events that merge into a timeless city of the mind, where the palaces of the Caesars track those of the Renaissance and the Fascists.

Berlusconi was presumably in no mood for sightseeing. After meeting briefly with the president, he fled the palace

Berlusconi on the night of his resignation (2011)

through a side door, where the awaiting Audi whisked him to safety.

The latest of his extensive legal woes included accusations of soliciting sex from an underage Moroccan prostitute who called herself Ruby Rubacuore (Ruby the Heart Stealer), which led to yet another of the numerous trials he has faced since first taking office in 1994. But matters were even worse for the thousands in the triumphant crowd. Italy was mired in an economic free fall, with unemployment spiking to 10 percent (as high as 50 percent for young people in the south) and a catastrophic credit crisis. The day of Berlusconi's resignation, Italy's economy—eighth largest in the world—held $2.6 trillion in debt, 120 percent of its GDP.

Brain drain, Bribe City, *crescita zero* ("zero birth rate"), *mammoni, paese di merda* ("shit hole," Berlusconi's own term), Xenophobic Nation—these are just a few choice epithets now associated with the Bel Paese, the "Beautiful Land." Not a day passes, it seems, without some dark omen as the nation struggles with an aging population, deadening bureaucracy, rising unemployment, and endless corruption. A full third of Italians don't pay taxes. The Northern League wants to secede from the union. The Mafia flourishes in the south. Boatfuls of illegal immigrants drown trying to reach Italy. Garbage piles up in Naples. The captain of the *Costa Concordia* abandons—or is accidentally thrown from—his ship. Nothing can escape the alarm and decay, not even the family jewel: the city of Venice, which welcomes about twenty million visitors a year, continues to sink into the Adriatic. Ravaged by floods that erode the foundations of its buildings, the Serenissima has lost most of its inhabitants to in-

Death in Venice: a mock funeral

dustrial, mainland Mestre and its teeming shopping malls. In 1950 the population of Venice stood at 150,000; it is now about 50,000. *The Guardian* recently estimated that by 2046, the city could be left without native inhabitants—a grim reality that inspired Venetians to hold a mock funeral for their dying city, its glory days a distant memory.

Berlusconi became prime minister for the first time in 1994, the year I started graduate school and a year before my father's death. The Italy I had come to know—the northern land of my adult life that had followed my southern Italian childhood—was much the creation of the man in the armored Audi. I decided to go to Italy and see which of my two Italies was still standing.

•

Shortly after Berlusconi's resignation I attended the panel "Italy Today: Politics, Culture, and the Economy," at the American Academy in Rome. The event brought together some of the leading analysts of contemporary Italian life. The director of the American Academy, Christopher Celenza, began by noting that "all of us who are living in Italy must recognize that we're in a time of great change—or at least great *apparent* change." The NPR correspondent Sylvia Poggioli organized her remarks around Italy's "long-drawn-out social and moral crisis," and the sociologist David Kertzer described the pessimism that has plagued Italian politics since the *anni di piombo*, the terrorist "years of lead" in the 1970s. Rachel Donadio of *The New York Times* summed up the complexity of the situation: "It's very hard to follow what's going on in Italy at this moment. We've kind of gone from talking about bunga bunga [Berlusconi's allegedly Nero-like bacchanals] to *ammortizzatore sociale*" ("social security cushion"), a form of unemployment insurance.

Donadio was right—it would take a Dante to fathom the muddle that has become life in contemporary Italy. No character in the *Inferno* combines everything that Berlusconi has been brought to trial for, if not convicted of: bribery, Mafia collusion, false accounting, tax evasion, government corruption, and sexual solicitation. And Italy's scandals aren't limited to the upper echelons of government. Each day, thousands evade taxes, rig bids, work under the table, give relatives preferential treatment, and engage in other illicit activities that have earned Italy its reputation as a place where virtue goes to die (the European Union listed Italy as second only to near-bankrupt Greece in corruption).

I had arrived that spring of 2012 anticipating a much different Italy from the one I had known. The nation was in the ongoing grip of a devastating financial crisis, and Mario Monti's transitional government faced enormous challenges. Much of the country's unemployed youth refused to accept the adult challenges of marriage and parenting, and droves of highly skilled workers were abandoning their country for greater opportunities abroad. I expected to see, if not blood in the streets, at least chaos and fear. What I found instead was the usual withering cynicism and pasta-induced lethargy. If Italy was dying, it would do so on a full stomach and in the middle of a peaceful afternoon nap.

After the panel I joined the speakers for dinner at the American Academy. Seated next to me, a journalist who had covered the terrorist years of the 1970s railed against his nation.

"Non hai idea," he kept repeating, "You have no idea" how much people like him had sacrificed for what they all believed would one day be a better Italy.

My exposure to the nation's crisis that spring was limited to Rome and the cosmopolitan world of the academy. Still, I had spent enough time traveling throughout the country and talking with people in different walks of life to realize that the end was not at hand. Life in Italy was churning along much as it had when I first arrived there in 1987. Just how little it had changed became clear after a visit to the post office.

As always, I relished the chance to buy books in Italy and mail them home to avoid lugging them through the airport. When I told my plan to the staff at the American Academy, they broke into smothered laughs and gave me sympathetic looks usually reserved for someone about to undergo a root canal or renew his license. I wasn't surprised: the post office is Italy's version of the DMV, home to the nation's most spiteful and least accommodating workers. I didn't give the staff's reaction a second thought until one of them warned me that they wouldn't ship my books unless I wrapped them in the *modo standard*. In the freewheeling land of Armani's trim silhouettes and Leonardo's flying machines, you have to ship books in a box covered in brown wrapping paper and secured with a string. The whole production was one of those wastes of time so intense that they reduce you to a stupor—though I must admit that it did result in a lovely package.

I took my elegant box with me to the local post office. The line was the shortest I'd ever seen at the normally over-flowing *ufficio postale*, and my number flashed on the screen within minutes. After I deposited my package on the coun-ter, a large woman in her fifties with dyed hair asked me for my *codice fiscale*, "fiscal code," an ID assigned to each citizen and used to trace financial transactions. I told her that as a tourist and foreigner, I of course had no such number. She said sorry: no number, no delivery.

"You mean to tell me," I said, "that you can't mail a package in this country without a *codice fiscale*?"

She wasted no time in delivering the bureaucratic coup de grâce: she didn't make the rules, only followed them.

Her request meant that to mail a package, you had to be an Italian citizen or a business entity of some sort with ties to Italy. The situation confounded all logic and com-mon sense. I continued to argue with the woman (my irascible father would have been proud). She lurched forward in her seat—her upper torso seemed to have spontaneously generated from the berth of her stool—and tore into me one final time. *"Le ho detto, signore, non faccio le regole, le seguo soltanto"* ("I told you, mister, I don't make the rules, I only follow them"). I had to admit defeat.

Walking home, I cursed Italy's bloated bureaucracy and swore that I could never live in a country where whims masqueraded as laws. But halfway up the Via Carini, a thought calmed me. This was indeed the same Italy I first encountered in 1987, when I came to Florence for my junior year abroad. The lines were just as long, the dance between freewheeling corruption and mind-numbing regulation still as intricate and inscrutable. More important, I had my answer to the question that had been haunting me ever since I watched Berlusconi flee in his Audi: How could Italians have voted for him so often and for so long? This question was connected to a deeper one: Why had my parents left their poor but settled life in the Bel Paese for the uncertainty of America? The painted clerk on Via Carini provided my answer—and brought me back to one of the authors now filed in my beautifully wrapped box of books.

My health is good. I live here as in a hermitage; my books and my solitary walks take up all my time. My life is more monotonous than the movement of the stars, more colorless and insipid than a libretto of our opera.

Thus wrote Giacomo Leopardi, Italy's greatest modern poet, in 1823, during an extended stay at the estate of his noble family in Recanati. Thanks to Giacomo's diatribes, the town has become shorthand for provincial misery in Italy ("I was born to a noble family in an ignoble town," he once wrote). Recanati *is* Italy: the typical small town of close-knit families; the bell tower at the city center, ringing its tones like the heart pumping its blood; the hierarchies of noble and common, priest and peasant, merchant and migrant; and the feelings of local allegiance that align Italians in networks of family, guild, client, and clan. Italy, Leopardi understood, has always been a massive team sport.

This localism inspired the hunchback Leopardi, nearly blind from the years of nonstop reading that began in his

Giacomo Leopardi in a collage by Terry Castle (2010)

childhood, to write one of the darkest pieces of his painful
life: the *Discourse on the Present State of the Customs of the Italians*, composed in 1824 during the time he spent at home
with books as his lone companions. Leopardi wrote that Italy's fundamental problem was a lack of "society": it had no
sense of national community to unite its people, no public
sphere that regulated conduct and taste and gave rise to sentiments of honor and shame. According to Leopardi, Italians
were supreme individualists—fond of the public gesture and
charming act, but unwilling to foster group activity. We all
know, he writes, "that laws without customs are not enough,"
and that unlike other civic nations, Italians lack "great moral
principles." In Leopardi's view, this resistance to collective
thinking made Italians the most cynical of peoples, incapable of believing in the public good and unwilling to sacrifice
their private concerns.

This absence of society and civic culture helps account
for Berlusconi's meteoric rise. Because their political system
lacks strong traditions of sacrifice and patriotism, many Italians stood by idly as Berlusconi wreaked political havoc. Many
voters allowed this because they believed that his can-do
capitalism represented a break from the party politics that
had dominated Italian government from the 1940s to the
1990s, before it ended in the welter of corruptions known as
Tangentopoli or Bribe City. These voters, it turned out, were
right: Berlusconi *did* destroy the party system. But even the
most fanciful of his early supporters could not have predicted
the degree of turmoil his self-serving brand of populism
would engender.

The Italian ability to transform everyday life into an art
of living also provides clues about the rise of Berlusconi. Italy

is not just a country that produces beauty; it is defined by it. In Lampedusa's *The Leopard*, the title character explains the soul of his Sicilian people:

> Two or three days before Garibaldi entered Palermo I [the Leopard] was introduced to some British naval officers from one of the warships then in the harbor to keep an eye on things . . . They came to my house, I accompanied them up on to the roof; they were simple youths, in spite of their reddish whiskers. They were ecstatic about the view, the light; they confessed, though, that they had been horrified at the squalor and filth of the streets around. I didn't explain to them that one thing was derived from the other . . . Then one of them asked me what those Italian volunteers were really coming to do in Sicily. *"They are coming to teach us good manners,"* I replied in English. *"But they won't succeed, because we think we are gods."*

I had long puzzled over those words: *I didn't explain to them that one thing was derived from the other*—that the surpassing natural beauty of Sicily, its exquisite art and architecture, drew life from the surrounding poverty and squalor. I was no less confused by the closing remark: *because we think we are gods.* What kind of god, I wondered, could accept the marriage of beauty and filth, excellence and failure—the light of the stars and the stench of the gutter?

Those who think they're gods are likely to be punished for their pride—think of the Tower of Babel. Fittingly, over the years, the news of the world featured one disgraced Italian after another: captured mafiosi in cheap T-shirts;

impeccably tailored government ministers and bronzed businessmen on perp walks; Berlusconi leering at pretty passersby—and cracking raunchy jokes. No sector of society stood outside the corruption. Few would deny the sordid nature of much of Italian politics, but how does it derive from the land of Dante, Michelangelo, and Verdi, from a people renowned for their charm, grace, and spirit? This link, and the meaning of the Leopard's words, continued to escape me—until the recent scandal involving Berlusconi and Ruby the Heart Stealer.

In the midst of Rubygate, an Italian friend told me that at a bar in rural Tuscany she overheard some local pensioners rehashing Silvio's exploits. While an elderly man went on about the premier's alleged harem, the man's wife interjected, in a blunt Tuscan that would have impressed Dante, *"Ah, se capitasse a te, Giulio"* ("If only that could happen to you, Giulio"), a subjunctive testament to the prime minister's prowess in matters libidinal. The story of the horny old Tuscan contained a peculiar wisdom. Many Italians, from the political left, right, and center, would love to be as rich, powerful, and well sexed as Berlusconi (worth some $10 billion). Giulio was not alone in his jealousy. But something about the spectacle that Berlusconi offered Italians recalled Lampedusa's observation about the aesthetics of Italian life as well as Leopardi's vision of Italy as a nation without society.

With his face-lifts, seaside villas, Marinella ties, sprawling estates, and near-naked showgirls, Berlusconi embodies the Italian love of surfaces. Leopardi's cynical Italians have little sense of the public morality that led many Americans to condemn a president's infidelity, as they did during the Clinton-Lewinsky scandal. Like most Europeans, Italians don't expect their leaders to set examples of probity. In fact, they expect them to misbehave, as they have more opportunities for mischief, resources for deployment, and skill for deception than the run of the mill. But Italians also demand that when a leader strays, he should know how to avoid creating a scandal. The Berlusconi debacle was less about morality than about appearances: those who supported Berlusconi on the right were embarrassed by his behavior and wary of its implications. His opponents on the left saw an opportunity to attack a weakened adversary. Certainly a portion of the population felt moral outrage unmotivated by political intent, but most Italians are too skeptical, too worldly—in Leopardi's words, too cynical—to go that route.

Berlusconi transferred the fine art of being Italian into the political arena. A 2011 *New Yorker* piece by Ariel Levy noted, "[Berlusconi] has convinced Italians that he is someone they can both relate to and aspire to be like. Many men still feel that he is being attacked for being irresistible to women (which they would like to be) and plainly human, susceptible to sin (just like them). 'He's on the same wavelength as people,' one of Berlusconi's friends told me. 'He laughs when they laugh.'" In the spirit of the average citizen, Berlusconi likes what he likes (sex, money, power) and is not afraid to show it. The electorate prized him for nearly two decades because he made a show of scorning politics and projected an image of his "realness" all over the nation's televisions, newspapers, and computer screens (it didn't hurt that his company Mediaset owned most of Italy's communications industry). Disgusted by years of secretive government shaped by an inscrutable party structure, Italians couldn't get enough of his reality show. No wonder the Tuscan Giulio longed for a moment in Silvio's shoes.

The case of Berlusconi, with its fusion of Leopardi's lack of society and Lampedusa's beautiful surfaces, reveals how Italy's defects stem from its merits. We celebrate Italy for its beauty and expressiveness, but they come with a price. No two terms suggest the ambivalence—even melancholy—of Italy's art of living more than the untranslatable *sprezzatura* and *bella figura*. In a book written five hundred years ago but still relevant, Baldassare Castiglione's Renaissance etiquette manual, *The Book of the Courtier* (1528), describes *sprezzatura* as a studied carelessness that "conceals art and presents everything said and done as something brought about without laboriousness and almost without giving it any thought." Yet the apparent nonchalance masks hard work and careful preparation. *Sprezzatura* transcends mere style: it can reflect a true genius for living and savoir faire, the ability to handle complex matters with a light touch. It was precisely this capacity for lightness in Italian culture that inspired a gloomy, introspective northerner like Nietzsche to celebrate the Italian approach to life.

Bella figura is even more complicated. To be in its presence is to feel like you are the center of the world. Practitioners of *bella figura* will do the right thing: pay for your meal at dinner; drop everything to show you around town; remember your birthday; give a moving toast at your wedding; love your haircut; compliment you on that new shirt nobody else noticed. *Bella figura* entails a performance, in the calculating but not the crass sense of the word. In Italy, the art of living is an improvised spectacle. *Bella figura* ensures that the theater never closes.

The chiaroscuro art of Italian life mixes a flair for doing the right thing with a desire to be noticed, blurring the distinction between generosity and vanity. As the Leopard

MY TWO ITALIES

warns, you can't have one without the other—cannot have a nation obsessed with beautiful forms without the devotion to seductive appearances devoid of moral substance. As with much in Italian life, acts of *sprezzatura* and *bella figura* take place informally, beyond what Leopardi called the "bond and break" of actual law. Think of the unspoken rules that govern an Italian table: no grated cheese on seafood; never serve wine across someone's body; no mixing of *primi* and *secondi* dishes. These are among the few laws that Italians actually respect—ones that enrich the art of living rather than strengthen the ties that bind. In Italian society, as in the Italian language, it is better to be beautiful than good.

Sometimes that beauty can be terrible.

Soon after the *Costa Concordia*'s deadly shipwreck on January 18, 2012, Beppe Severgnini wrote in the *Financial Times*:

Why did the ship sail so close to Giglio and into its shallow waters? Because her captain, Mr. Schettino, wished to please chief steward Antonello Tievoli, whose family lives on the island. He proposed an *inchino* (a sail-past, literally a "bow" or "curtsy"): the huge cruiser—carrying more than 4,000 passengers and crew—would show up and show off, with lights glittering and sirens sounding . . . Once again, an Italian fell into the trap of *la bella figura*, this time, with tragic consequences. "La bella figura", the beautiful figure: only in Italian does such an expression exist. It means making "a good impression", in an aesthetic

sense. Too often, both in public and private, we con-
fuse what is beautiful with what is good . . . There is
a theatrical tendency in Italy, which is both part of
our charm and also at the root of our problems—and
not just on the high seas.

Bella figura, the beautiful act, the magnificent gesture—and
its utter lack of concern for the common good. Severgnini's
point recalled Leopardi's words. Just go to any Italian city
and watch the *passeggiata*, and you'll see how much Italians
love to be on display. In Naples, boys in black jeans swagger
past girls in sequined halter tops; in Siena, young couples in
khakis and cashmere sweaters push strollers around the Piazza del Campo. Everyone is making a *bella figura* of his own,
and it all looks good. Until someone gets hurt.

When the English poet Shelley wrote that there were
"two Italies," one sublime and the other odious, he wasn't just
representing the foreign view. Italians themselves are part *bella
figura* and part senseless regulation. Have old tires that you
need to get rid of? You need to contact a *gommista*, "tire spe-
cialist," and pay him handsomely. Want to repair the roof
of your shed? You'll have to ask a government agency for
permission. When you go to Italy for an extended stay, you
must present yourself to the local police. When I arrived in
1987, my roommates and I—red-blooded undergraduates—
were told that having overnight visitors would violate Italian
antiterrorism laws regarding unaccounted persons. Needless
to say, it was our own clumsiness, and not the desire to up-
hold the integrity of the national borders, that kept the *donne
italiane* from sleeping over.

Bella figura. Cynicism. No society. *Raccomandazioni*. These

well-worn traits created an unhealthy Italian body politic
in need of regulation. Italy is like the former party-hound
rock star reduced to pills and regimes that keep him alive
after decades of putting nasty things in his body—a Keith
Richards on Metamucil. Hence the millions of clerks, bu-
reaucrats, and other bean counters who generate the nation's
long lines and stacks of photocopied documents. For every
charming act of *bella figura* in Italy there is a nod to some
code or regulation. Lacking a public sphere, Italians responded with a stifling bureaucracy that counteracted the
political fragmention, foreign occupation, and every-*paesano*-
for-himself mentality. Each Italian has experienced his own
version of my post office crisis. Each probably yearned, as I
did that day on Via Carini, for someone powerful to do
away with the suffocating restrictions that sour so much of
the dolce vita.

After I told an Italian friend that I hadn't been allowed
to mail my books, he mentioned that there was an easy way
out of the mess.

"Just go online and get your *codice fiscale*. Here, I'll show
you how."

"But is that legal?" I asked, with no intention of entering my personal information into an Italian government
website.

"Well," he said with a smile, "let's just say it's a *Neapolitan*
solution to the probem." *Una soluzione alla napoletana.*

From 1994 to 2011, many Italians followed my friend's
lead and looked for a "Neapolitan" antidote to their nation's
woes—represented by the man who incarnated *bella figura*
and flashed a smile that promised to do away with each Italian's version of my wicked postal matron.

❋

My first year in Italy, I visited a wealthy classmate at his home in Milano 2, which the locals called "Milano Money" (it has also been labeled *la Beverly Hills italiana*). The enclave of sterile brick residences, which features a series of inter-connected walkways and a man-made Swan Lake, was like nothing I'd ever seen before in Italy. Surrounded by the quiet and order, I felt as if I'd landed in an upscale retirement community in Florida. Though I didn't know it at the time, Milano 2 also contained the nation's first independent cable television station—a perk to entice new residents. Several years later, in 1994, the man who created Milano Money was elected Italian prime minister for the first time. The cable channel in this yuppie development had been the first step in what would become Silvio Berlusconi's global media empire.

In the late 1980s Italy was still in its Cold War bureau-cratic age, which lasted from about 1947—the year of the most recent Italian constitution and the beginning of political dominance by the conservative Christian Democrat Party—to the bribery scandals of the early 1990s. During my first visit I opened a bank account with the help of a pretty, giggling Tuscan teller amid the marble of the Banco di Napoli on Via Cavour, one of the sleepy grand banks in Florence's *centro storico*. I was issued a bankbook with what felt like a fortune: one million lire, about $800. The nation's middle class had been enjoying high levels of prosperity since the 1960s. And in 1987 the economy achieved the unthinkable: *il sorpasso*, "the overtaking," when Italy passed Britain to become the world's fifth-largest economy. Suddenly it was one of the players.

The comfort took me by surprise: *Italy* and *poverty* had always been synonymous to me. My parents had described their homeland as a bleak terrain that abundant America had rescued them from. In truth, my parents left Italy just as the nation was entering its Economic Miracle, the boom years of postwar reconstruction in the late 1950s and 1960s. But this money didn't trickle down into my parents' Calabria until after they had emigrated. For a decade after their marriage, in 1946, they had tilled the land as corn, chestnut, and potato farmers and lived in a stone hut on a hill full of brambles. The sun pounded the brittle landscape, and there was no indoor plumbing. Their bathroom was nature itself, as they relieved themselves out in the woods, often using leaves as toilet paper. Their situation changed little when they first arrived in America. One Christmas, the only gifts my siblings received were new socks. Years later, as I ripped open the colored paper to find boxes of electronic goods and sporting equipment, I pitied them. But I also sensed that there was something noble in their forbearance. I knew that Christmas wasn't supposed to be about gifts, but my brothers and sisters had actually lived this preachy maxim. They talked about the delicious food they ate on those frugal Christmases, the games they played together out in the snow. And they didn't need a Mattel Electronics Hockey game or Donnay Borg Pro tennis racquet to remind them of the miracle of Christ's birth.

The impoverished Calabria of my parents had disappeared by the 1980s. During my initial visit in 1987, I met my cousins Giuseppe and Armando at their respective gas stations in the center of Cosenza. Their brother Angelo owned his own hardware store. Their net worth obviously dwarfed my own (and probably still does). Their father, my uncle

Giorgio, lived in Montalto Uffugo in a tiny house near the railroad tracks, where passing engines rattled me awake every few hours on those long, miserable nights I slept there. But Giorgio was from the generation of his sister Yolanda, my mother. His spare economic existence only verified his authenticity as a real Calabrian, while his nouveaux riches sons harnessed the ongoing energy of Italy's Economic Miracle.

I came to Italy in the 1980s to study art, not politics. Though I majored in political science as an undergraduate, at the time I knew little about the Italian government. I had no idea that in 1987, the prime minister was the Socialist Bettino Craxi, one of the most powerful men of postwar Italy, a political mentor of the young Berlusconi, who would flee to Tunis to avoid facing trial for corruption. Craxi's successor as premier was another political giant, Amintore Fanfani, a former Fascist and principal architect of the 1947 constitution that resurrected Italy after the fall of Mussolini. Worst of all, I didn't know that just a decade before my arrival, Italy had undergone one of the most painful political assassinations in modern history—an event whose implications would contribute to the election of Berlusconi.

On March 16, 1978, a cell of the Marxist-Leninist political terrorists called the Red Brigades kidnapped Aldo Moro, secretary of the Christian Democrats. Moro was one of the most influential men in this most influential of parties. He had been prime minister five times and in 1978 had begun to orchestrate a controversial Historic Compromise: the agreement between the Christian Democrats and Communists that would give the latter group key government positions in exchange for their pledge not to vote against Christian Democratic platforms. Moro's tactical brilliance and penchant for compromise made him as many enemies as friends. Many of the Christian Democrats reviled any rapprochement whatsoever with the dreaded, godless Communists, whose headquarters were appropriately located in the proletarian-sounding—though in fact patrician—Via delle Botteghe Oscure (Street of the Dark Shops). Likewise, more radical Communist groups such as the Red Brigades refused to deal with the capitalist, opiate-peddling (that is, religious) Christian Democrat Party, which was based, fittingly, in Piazza del Gesù (Jesus Square).

The Moro Affair is the Italian equivalent of the JFK assassination. Any Italian of a certain age remembers the exact place and time in which he heard the words *Moro è stato rapito*, "Moro has been kidnapped." He was taken to a hidden location of the Red Brigades somewhere in Rome, and the five members of his bodyguard were killed defending him. The Red Brigades announced that they were putting Moro on trial under the auspices of what they called "The People's Court of Justice." They found him guilty and sentenced him to death. They also agreed, however, to free him in exchange for the release of Red Brigades members held as prisoners. Moro begged Italian officials to accept this offer. Such trades, he claimed (correctly), were common in this type of situation.

Moro wrote letter after letter to those he believed were his friends among the Christian Democrats, including Prime Minister Giulio Andreotti and Minister of the Interior Francesco Cossiga. He also appealed to the pope and the secretary general of the United Nations, Kurt Waldheim. But the Italian government, largely under Andreotti's directive, adopted an uncooperative stance: no negotiations with the terrorists under any circumstances. Meanwhile, the manhunt was handled with breathtaking inefficiency by the police. One week. A few more weeks. Over a month. Finally, after fifty-one days, on May 5, the Red Brigades announced, "We conclude the battle started on March 16, by executing the sentence to which Aldo Moro was condemned." Four days later, a passerby noticed a smell coming from the trunk of a car on Via Caetani. It was Moro's corpse—symbolically parked halfway between the Communist and Christian Democrat headquarters.

The Moro case contains in a grotesque nutshell many of the characteristics that have marred Italian politics since unification: its factional multiparty system; the strange marriage between politics and religion in a nation where the church remains powerful; the partisanship that trumps public service; and the proverbial *trasformismo*, "transformism," that seeks to retain power at all costs. This mix of pragmatism and cynicism is summed up in Lampedusa's *The Leopard* when the young nobleman Tancredi Falconeri announces on the eve of the revolution, *"Se vogliamo che tutto rimanga come è, bisogna che tutto cambi"* ("If we want things to stay as they are, things will have to change"). For the nobles to retain their power, they had to feign support for the popular unification movement and then reposition themselves after the homages to liberty and democracy had been declared.

Though quite different from Berlusconi's political career, the Moro Affair reveals the secret of his ascent: the machinations of the Italian party system, which would implode

in the Tangentopoli era of the 1990s and make Italians
clamor for someone like Berlusconi. But the powerful busi-
nessman Berlusconi also enjoyed many cozy connections
with the party system he was thought to reject—especially
in his friendship with his mentor Craxi, who helped him
secure important licenses in the early stages of his media
conglomerate.

The story of Berlusconi goes back even further than
Moro. By the late 1940s, after a war that had sent my father
into the arms of his German captor, Italians were exhausted
by the warfare and repression associated with Mussolini's
cult-of-personality politics. So they established a system of
rigidly organized political parties as the administrative heart
of the nation. The party that emerged as first among equals,
the Christian Democrats, exploited the rampant fear of Com-
munism and drew the Italian public to their free-market and
family-oriented principles. The United States played its role
in propping up the Christian Democrats, pumping millions
of dollars into the nation through the Marshall Plan, one of
whose aims was to suppress the powerful Italian Communist
Party. Indeed, after World War II, many Western leaders
feared that Italy would "go red": the Communists had been
one of the few groups to challenge Mussolini during the *ven-
tennio*, the two decades of Fascist rule, from 1922 to 1943. But
when political push came to shove, the majority of Italians
could not embrace the platform of the extreme left, and they
chose instead the tradition-minded Christian Democrats.

The subsequent turn of events produced surprising results: the Economic Miracle raised Italian standards of living
dramatically, enabling the Christian Democrats to dominate
the legislature for much of the first fifty years after World

War II. This shift from a left-wing program founded on the struggles of the proletariat to the glittering Made in Italy look is documented in the nation's cinema: in 1948 the Marxist Luchino Visconti shot *La Terra Trema* on location in Sicily, using actual fisherman as his actors in a film devoted to exposing the inequalities faced by the working-class poor. But just a generation later, a politically indifferent Federico Fellini trained his lens on the beautiful people of Rome's Via Veneto in *La Dolce Vita* (1960), to reveal a rebuilt nation where the Alfa Romeos hummed and the Campari poured. The image of Italy was born.

The decades that followed would not be so glamorous. The 1970s earned the epithet *anni di piombo*, "years of lead," because of the amount of bullets fired during this time. Moro was one of the many victims of terrorism, which culminated in the *Strage di Bologna*, "Slaughter of Bologna," in the summer of 1980, when a neofascist group detonated explosives on a crowded train of beachgoers, killing eighty. From 1983 to 2001 the country endured no less than sixteen different executive administrations (one lasted only eleven days). Despite the shuffling of wing tips, a remarkable stability—or stagnancy—prevailed, with the same names surfacing and resurfacing. Andreotti served as prime minister seven times; Craxi held the top post three times.

By the 1990s the party structure was crumbling. During the Bribe City scandals, hundreds of politicians and thousands of professionals were brought to justice for misconduct and abuses of power. The Italian nation, already profoundly skeptical toward its government, was disgusted by the corruption that they linked to the party system. Italians were looking for a nonpartisan, a nonpolitician, an outsider who

could rescue them from deadening bureaucracy, corrupt administration, and a sclerotic business climate. A man who
would place Italy before party. A man powerful enough to
avoid the fate of Aldo Moro. A man whose personal fortune
and private interests would place him above the petty squab-
bles that had degraded the party system. Heeding the call, a
captain of industry from Milan announced that he was ready
to step forth and save his country.

On January 26, 1994, after studying the Italian political situation with a group of his managers, publicists, and other
business associates, Silvio Berlusconi distributed a 9-minute,
24-second videotape to the major media outlets in Italy (many
of which he owned). The recording included the following:

> Italy is the country I love. Here I have my roots, my
> hopes, my horizons. Here I have learned, from my
> father and from life, how to be an entrepreneur. Here
> I have acquired my passion for liberty . . . Never as
> in this moment [has] Italy . . . [needed] people of a
> certain experience, with their heads on their shoul-
> ders, able to give the country a helping hand and to
> make the state function.

After a meteoric rise as a real estate developer—thanks largely
to his showpiece property Milano 2—the former cruise-ship
crooner Silvio Berlusconi was elected prime minister from
his Forza Italia, "Go Italy," party, named after the cheer for
Italy's national soccer team. Berlusconi even called his parliamentarians *azzurri* (the color "blue," a reference to the uni-

form of the Italian national soccer team), described political engagement as "walking onto the field," and set up party headquarters in the former fan clubs of the AC Milan soccer team, which he owned.

Berlusconi always understood that in this virtual age, image is everything. He once returned from a three-week hiatus with a *lifting*, "face-lift," that erased the creases from his famous grin and the bags from beneath his sparkling salesman's eyes. Many of his ministers and political aides were former business associates, and much of his appeal derived from his promise to bring American-inspired capitalist reform and an entrepreneurial spirit to a land plagued by bureaucracy, heavy taxation, and fiscal conservatism.

Much has already been written about the former premier, his notorious gaffes, irrepressible sexuality, and ongoing political altercations. Less understood is how his policies affected the actual lives of the millions of Italians who either supported or condemned him during his nearly two decades in power. When I visited Rome in 2012, I made a point of asking people to name the one particular quality that made Berlusconi so irresistible for so long and to so many Italian voters. Each person had a different take. For some, it was his Citizen Kane–like control of the media. For others, it was his salesman's ability to convince anyone of anything. For most, it was his vast fortune that bankrolled his rise to the top. Frustrated by the variety of explanations, I decided to take my question to a professional politician—someone who, like Berlusconi, understood the Machiavellian necessities of life in public office. Someone who would be less likely to offer the usual moral critique of his foibles. If I was going to get the last word on Berlusconi, I wanted it to come from a statesman who had battled him directly and stared into his smiling eyes as an equal. I arranged to speak with the last person to defeat Berlusconi in a national election.

The office of Romano Prodi, the fifty-second and fifty-sixth prime minister of the Italian Republic (1996–1998, 2006–2008), occupies a sparse suite of rooms in the apartment next door to his home in the university district of Bologna, where Prodi has taught industrial relations since 1978. The modest decor made me wonder how this unassuming scholar—nicknamed Valium, for his quiet demeanor, as well as mortadella, a soft local cold cut—could have defeated the flamboyant Berlusconi and his legendary powers of seduction. I began my interview by asking Prodi what he thought of Leopardi's comment that Italy lacked society.

"Eravamo i leader nel Rinascimento" ("We were leaders in the Renaissance"), he said, describing that period as the "first globalization." But eventually, he continued, *la frammentazione*, "the fragmentation," set in. The Italian nation that was formed in 1861 was a weak one. "Italy is a society used to losing and being subjugated," he added.

I asked him why, in the midst of all the challenges it has been facing, Italy turned to Berlusconi.

"In a time of great crises," he said, referring to the Tangentopoli scandals of the early 1990s and the collapse of the Italian political party system, "the nation entrusted itself to someone outside of the usual political traditions." It was a "desperate act." He went on to emphasize Berlusconi's charisma as a *grande venditore*, "great salesman." It would be snobbish to underestimate Berlusconi, Prodi said, for he has a "nuclear option":

his control of the media as well as the support of the economic establishment. "As his political opponent," he said, "I can assure you that the power of the media was incredible." Manipulating his vast communications network, Berlusconi offered Italians *"il sogno del successo facile"* ("the dream of easy success") and *"il sogno della bellezza"* ("the dream of beauty").

I told Prodi my own theory as to why Berlusconi was able to reach such soaring political heights: Italians believed he would free them from the crushing bureaucracy embodied by the wicked postal matron on Via Carini who refused to mail my package of books. He smiled and said that Berlusconi's original party, Forza Italia, was *"il partito di quelli che vogliono parcheggiare in seconda fila"* ("the party of those who want to double park").

Throughout our interview Prodi kept noticing my iPhone, which I was using to record our conversation. I concluded by asking him if Italy's celebrated high culture could play a role in helping the nation out of its malaise. He told me the story of a Chinese student who had asked him if Europe was *"un laboratorio o un museo"* ("a laboratory or a museum"). Prodi said that the question applied particularly to Italy, then spoke of the inventions that had transformed life in the past twenty-five years: the computer, the fax, the flat-screen television—and yes, the smartphone.

"Not one has been invented or produced in Italy," he said in English. "This is my nightmare."

He ended our conversation by quoting Dante: *"Fatti non foste a viver come bruti, ma per seguir virtute e canoscenza,"* the famous motto in *Inferno* 26 uttered by Ulysses to his crew: "You were not made to live like brutes or beasts, but to pursue virtue and knowledge." When Italians want to pursue virtue and knowledge, Prodi remarked, they go abroad.

Before leaving, I mentioned that I'd spent most of my time in Italy in Florence, and I wondered whether this Renaissance city that I loved so deeply could have a modern afterlife. Whether, to use Prodi's own words, it could become a laboratory or would remain a museum. He wasted no time in replying:

"Firenze è un museo."

In 1818, the first year of his Italian exile, the English poet Shelley—the same man who had described the two Italies, one sublime and the other odious—offered his initial impressions of Rome:

> Rome is a city, as it were, of the dead, or rather of those who cannot die, and who survive the puny generations which inhabit and pass over the spot which they have made sacred to eternity. In Rome, at least in the first enthusiasm of your recognition of ancient time, you see nothing of the Italians.

When I wrote about this passage a decade ago, I criticized Shelley for his typically mystifying foreign view. How on earth could he call a city with a population of more than a hundred thousand—one of the most populous in Italy and Europe—"dead"? And why did he turn a blind eye to the local literary culture that might have appealed to a brilliant Italianist like himself, as works by such major authors as Goldoni, Alfieri, and Foscolo filled the bookshops of the Eternal City? "Shelley's interests," I wrote, "lay not with Italy's living. In his eyes—or at least in the 'first enthusiasm' of his encounter with Rome's 'ancient time'—the cultural moment of the Italian past obscured 'the puny generations' in its wake." Fair enough. But what I did not know at the time—what I could not know, because my study of Italy was confined to books and not the living culture of Italians—was that Shelley was right: Rome was indeed a city of the dead. Only a poet could measure the population of "those who cannot die," not a demographer, and certainly not a scholar like me, who ignored the spirit behind Shelley's words.

During my time in Rome in 2012, a series of cab rides made me think back to those remarks at the American Academy about contemporary Italy. One of the cabbies, who drove a sleek Mercedes sedan, believed that the political parties "took money" and that the technocratic Prime Minister Monti was *"prendendo in giro"* ("tricking") Italians with his "false government." I asked a second cabdriver if he thought Monti was doing a good job, and he said no—unless, of course, you were lucky enough to be in the *"ceto benestante"* ("the well-to-do set"). Another cabbie echoed his colleagues: the austerity measures put into place by the new administration were crippling the working and middle classes while leaving the wealthy and well connected untouched. Of course, people throughout the world—and cabdrivers in particular— love to complain about those in charge, and they can solve the world's problems over a ten-dollar fare. But the relentless tone of pessimism astonished me. With their sharp critiques of Italian public life, the cabbies might have been channeling Leopardi, Prodi, and the American Academy panel.

Prodi once wrote that Italians have "tactics" but "no final goal." Leopardi went further and said that Italians were incapable of respecting moral principles when self- or group interests came into play. The deadness that Shelley perceived in Rome was a combination of, on the one hand, the political and social inertia, and on the other, the mausoleum-like magnificence of the city's art and architecture. Most days in Rome, a research trip took me down from the Janiculum Hill to the city center by taxi. The car would converge upon one of the world's most beautiful traffic circles, the cobblestones of Piazza Venezia, where the ruins of antiquity, the palaces of the Renaissance, and the clean lines of modern design coalesce under what are usually cloudless blue skies. Even among the choking exhaust and fumes, this world of gorgeous objects crowds out the living.

But again, the beauty comes with a price. Nathaniel Hawthorne described Rome as a "marble wilderness," and the society inhabiting this landscape of monuments is just as immobile. Shelley saw no living Italians in Rome, because public life there remained far less dynamic, far more prone to fragmentation and self-interest than in his native England. My cabdrivers said it best when they unanimously voiced their disbelief that any real change would occur in the country. Surrounded by rapturous works of art and nailed to the cross of the dolce vita, the Romans I met in 2012, like the Florentines in the 1980s and the Calabrians in the 1990s, resigned themselves to a marble wilderness filled with corrupt leaders and lacking a civil society.

After Florence exiled Dante in 1302, he described Italy in *The Divine Comedy* as a "brothel" that let in foreigners for the right price and allowed greed and other vices to ruin the nation. It took Italy six hundred years after Dante's birth to become unified, and now many fear that this divided nation may collapse under financial and political pressure. I doubt that Armageddon awaits resilient Italy, but we should keep in mind Shelley's words. Even more than the troubled aftermath of Berlusconi and the fraught transition under Monti, what struck me in Rome in 2012 was the leaden atmosphere of the taxis, cafés, and lecture halls of the Eternal City. The greatest fear was not that things would get worse or that sacrifices would need to be made, but rather, to quote Tancredi from *The Leopard*, that things would change only in order to stay the same. The great Dante scholar Erich Auerbach said that here lies the pathos of Dante's hell: its sinners don't change; they are fixed forever in the act that undid them. This is real death, the one that leads to neither redemption nor closure, merely repetition. This is why Shelley called warm, wine-soaked Rome the city where death lives—and why my mother and father abandoned everyone they loved for a foreign land far from the Mezzogiorno and its delirious midday sun.

6

Florence After Florence

In 1987, I arrived at JFK Airport with $1,400 in travelers checks rolled into my zippered belt. I had just turned twenty and was about to board a flight to Rome, my first international trip—and my first visit to Italy. All around me, college students in skinny jeans tugged at the earphones of Sony Discman players perched on their limp hair. Many of them already knew one another from such places as Oberlin and SUNY Purchase, so they made the rounds while I stood by in my crew cut and Le Coq Sportif tennis shirt. I was about to begin my junior year abroad, an undeserved gift after two undistinguished academic years. I lacked the study habits of the A student and the free spirit of the C one, so I muddled through with B's, dutiful enough to hand in my work, but clueless about what I was supposed to do at college.

In truth, I almost quit before I began. When my parents dropped me off for the chicken sandwich spread at Tufts University's freshman orientation in 1985, I wandered around among the kids from Newton and Scarsdale, Nyack and Short Hills who reminisced about their summer camps and corporate internships. My own summers had been spent making knitted pot holders and necklaces at the local playground, and instead of poring over briefs, I cut lawns and bagged groceries. I had never spent a night away from home before college. With my family gone all of an hour, my body trembled with homesickness.

That first week before classes I moped about campus and fantasized about winning back the girl who had dumped me on the night of the senior prom in the elevator of the Biltmore Hotel in Providence on our way up to the ballroom. I wanted to go back home—to what, I had no idea. Just as long as it took me away from this beautiful brick campus and its worldly students. And just as long as I never had to sleep another night in my brutalist dorm with its nauseating smell of fresh white paint. I called home and told my sister Rose, whom my father had not allowed to go to college because she was *'na fimmina*, "a woman," that I wanted out. "If you come back," she said quietly—she had inherited my father's ability to drive a spike into your heart with a soft word—"you'll be making the biggest mistake of your life. Don't you dare." I stayed put. But the fog never lifted, and I spent the first two years wandering around this liberal arts paradise in desperate need of a map.

I thought that Italy would provide the missing guidance. Throughout sophomore year I stared at the brochure of the art school where I would be studying. Florence at dusk, bathed in pink and orange, the saturated light of the study-abroad dream . . . I would fall in love in Italy. Some raven-haired Italian girl named Donatella would explain to me the mysteries of Perugino's red- and green-gowned ladies. I would be able to say, in the legendary words attributed to

Correggio, *"Anch'io son pittore,"* "I too am a painter"—even though I'd yet to pick up a brush.

Freshman year at Tufts, I shared a dorm with one of the campus's international beauties, Giselda from Turin. She was rail thin, she chain-smoked, and she seemed to know her way around a Swiss après ski. Light skinned and as sleek as a Ferrari, she stood worlds apart from the thick, black-haired women I had grown up with. She was a real European—and she let me know it. When I told her that my parents and older siblings were born in Italy, in Calabria, she snorted. "That's Africa," she said, "not Italy." I was twice degraded in her eyes: not a real American, like the kids from Choate and Collegiate who tooled around campus in their Mazda convertibles and Volvo wagons, and definitely not Italian, with my dark hair, dark eyes, and increasingly dark world-view. My year abroad was not a program of study; it was a cry for help.

I longed for a room with a view. I got budget traveler. The shutters in my Piazza della Libertà bedroom shook from the traffic below, as the city's ring roads converged just outside my window. My first night in Florence I walked with my roommates away from the noise and onto the elegant Via Cavour. The Duomo appeared in the gloaming. Its scale flabbergasted me: I felt its massive egg shape absorbing the surrounding buildings. It was the heart of the city—the only heart Florence would ever reveal to me, the bloodless one of monuments.

The boardinghouse feel of my lodgings (six students in three small bedrooms) and the meager facilities of my program (the library consisted of a few paperbacks and volumes of artists' reproductions) intensified my homesickness. I ate my first meal in one of the city's many overrated restaurants, in the workman's quarter near the Mercato di San Lorenzo, home to a thriving black market in leather goods. At the time, the now-corporate Trattoria Zà Zà hadn't decided whether to serve honest food to locals or sell its soul to the tourist dollar. Day after day I showed up there for heaping bowls of *spaghetti al pesto*, a green pine-nut sauce that was off-limits in my stewed-tomato childhood. The sharp, earthy aroma opened my nostrils, and the basil punched through the heavy starch. It felt comforting, but it did not feel like home.

Those first months, I walked around the monuments with two souls as lost as I was: Alexis, a thin, neurotic Greek American painter from D.C., and Anthony, a budding art historian, with a teenage mustache, a New Jersey accent (he pronounced our host country "IT-lee"), and black patent leather shoes. His family must have had serious working-class money: while the other unwashed students loaded up on pizza, panini, and wine in straw bottles, Anthony wore a tuxedo jacket on our art history trips and invited Alexis and me to restaurants with starched white tablecloths. This was no academic trip for Anthony; it was a pilgrimage. One day in a museum in Rome he stood beside me with quivering lips as he contemplated a large Renaissance canvas. "That's my AN-cest-uh," he murmured in an ecstasy approaching Raphael's ravished Saint Catherine.

I wrote letters home saying how thrilled I was to be in the Old Country. I knew how fortunate I was to have a full year of student leisure while my parents struggled in their vacation- (and vocation-) free world. How blessed I was to stroll the northern Italian cobblestones when my siblings only ever knew the Calabrian dust and Rhode Island asphalt. But in truth I was sick to my stomach: sick of the pesto, of the misfit company of Alexis and Anthony, of the horns and sirens of Piazza della Libertà. I considered cutting my study abroad in half and returning to the United States for the spring semester.

Then I bought a ticket to the ancestral home.

At first the train ride to Calabria was no different from the others I had taken to points north, with the same leather bags, silk scarves, and *la Repubblica* and *Corriere della Sera* newspapers of fellow travelers who filled the compartments for six that were designed for casual but meaningful conversation. Occasionally a ticket inspector would slide open the door and interrupt the chatter, as the hills of Tuscany and Lazio rolled by. Once we reached Naples, however, the terrain turned brown and rocky, and the teenagers with books under their noses detrained, giving up their seats to girls with puckered lips and boys with moussed hair. Low-slung families with three or four children piled into the compartments with plastic bags bursting with tomatoes, salami, cheese, and yogurt. At Napoli Centrale, I switched from the silent, cheetah-like Intercity to a mechanical brontosaurus that lumbered from one nondescript town to the next. It took hours after leaving Naples to cover the few hundred miles to Cosenza, my family's homeland.

I came with an address: the gas station where my cousin Armando worked. I showed up and told him who I was: *"Giuseppe Luzzi, il figlio di Yolanda e Pasquale Luzzi."* He gave me a half-bemused, half-suspicious look and placed a few calls—whether to announce my arrival or verify my identity, I don't know. Then his more trusting brother Giuseppe came from his own gas station and escorted me to see his parents, my uncle Giorgio and aunt Filomena. Within two hours of arriving, I was eating *pastasciutta al pomodoro*, "pasta in tomato sauce," in a stucco house with an outdoor bathroom in the village of Montalto Uffugo.

I spent the next day in the elevated *centro storico* of Cosenza, photographing old women and their straw broomsticks amid the ancient city streets my parents had walked in their youth. Giuseppe took me on a pilgrimage to *"u voscu"* (*"il bosco,"* "the woods"), the remote forested area in the countryside outside Cosenza that even for my impoverished parents represented the final word in hard living. I met two distant relatives, a middle-aged woman and her wizened mother. Their rotten teeth, sackcloth clothes, and complete ignorance of the wider world made my parents seem like sophisticates. I heard from a villager who carried a knife about how the local Mob, the 'Ndrangheta, stopped by businesses like his each week for their *bustarella*, the "envelope" stuffed with protection money.

Meanwhile, I kept stealing glances at an advertisement of a long-limbed woman in a blue hip-hugging dress that I had torn out of an Italian fashion magazine in Florence. I wanted desperately to paint her. Back in Florence. Staid, graceful Florence. Suddenly the trip abroad made sense, and the homesickness began to melt away. I had work to do, art to see, Alexis and Anthony to abandon. After a farewell meal with Giorgio and Filomena, I boarded the train at Cosenza and began the long journey north to that *altra Italia*, other Italy.

Back in Florence, I called the woman at Tufts I'd been dating to say that I wasn't going to come home for the holidays as planned. To place the call, I had to go to the public phone booths in Piazza della Repubblica, where sweaty men in blue short-sleeve shirts called your number and directed you to one of the available cabins. By the time the call ended, the meter had ticked off 70,000 lire or $50, an astronomical sum for me. It was past midnight, and on the way back to my apartment I stopped in the empty Piazza della Signoria and sat by the haunches of Ammannati's beefcake Neptune. The hands on the clock tower of the Palazzo Vecchio were fixed in their usual position, as if to emphasize that nothing new ever happened in Florence. I looked up at the statue. Neptune's face was set in its habitual glare. *Get yourself together,* I felt him say.

Within a month I had moved out of Piazza della Libertà, cut ties with Alexis and Anthony, settled into an apartment with an enormous terrace near the soccer stadium, and finished the first painting of my life: a model in a blue dress, with what looked like dislocated hips, her lines as long as the spine separating Florence from Cosenza.

I spent much of the next twenty years studying, teaching, traveling, and living in Florence—but I never got closer to it than that junior year abroad. I had landed there in 1987 expecting the Merchant-Ivory version, but found instead a noisy city filled with stale bread and trinket shops selling Duomo lighters and ashtrays. Yet even in that first disillusioning visit, I knew why I had come. If I could make Florence my home, then nobody could ever accuse me of being more

African than Italian—of being a *terrone*, a "muddy peasant," the racist slur used to describe southern Italians. Wil-
lowy Giselda didn't have to utter that word to let me know
she meant it. Florence, I believed, would enable me to up-
grade from my parents' Calabria to a calzone-free Italian
lineage.

Despite my many visits, the Florentines continued to regard me as a tourist. I longed for what I imagined to be their
magical world: excursions to a country estate for the first
wine of the year; gallery openings across the Arno in the
shadow of Santo Spirito; family dinners in the Liberty-style
flats of the stately Piazza Beccaria. I taught their culture and
had devoted my life to publicizing their art to the world. Yet
the Florentines held their ground. No matter how much my
Italian improved, no matter how often I wore that slim-
waisted Montezemolo shirt with the bold stripe, I could not
scale the barriers to entry. Instead I spent my days with colleagues at the city's libraries and archives, socialized with
fellow Americans, and continued to live in the Italy of can-
vases, statues, and columns.

At times the city felt like a prostitute—*come and enjoy
yourself, cash up front, no kissing.* Other times, a long-suffering
mistress—*if you really loved me, you'd spend the holidays with me.*
Once, as the director of my college's study abroad program
in Florence, I thought of moving my students to another
city. Halfway through negotiations with a group from
Parma, I stopped: I felt as if I were cheating on Florence,
stuck at home with the kids while I sought a less prickly
companion.

•

Things came to a head in 2005, when I had left my teaching at Bard College for a year's fellowship at the National Humanities Center in North Carolina. I traded my cramped railroad apartment in Brooklyn for a cavernous loft in one of Durham's refurbished tobacco warehouses and set about preparing for a life together with Katherine. The night she joined me in North Carolina, we had dinner at the Magnolia Grill in Durham after walking through Duke's east campus to Whole Foods, which would supply a year of feasts that nourished our growing love. After nine months together during my residency at the National Humanities Center, I was planning to leave her for the summer, to take my annual trip to Florence. The midnight before my flight, after a steak dinner and many glasses of wine together, I still hadn't finished packing. I woke up at five thirty a.m. with a searing headache. I went for an aspirin, but fumbled with the jar and ended up spilling the capsules all over the bathroom floor. My insides seized in panic.

"I don't feel like going," I whispered to Katherine as she slept.

I dialed Alitalia and asked about the penalties for canceling my flight. A representative named Angelo explained the fees I would incur. I started to do the math but pulled back before finishing the equation. I thought of all the people I had told I was going: trusted colleagues, foreign friends, admired mentors. What would they think? Right when the woman I loved depended on me to do something brave—I won't say manly—I played it safe. I hung up on Angelo, scooped the pills off the floor, and kissed Katherine goodbye.

The next day, I found myself in Florence for the summer—the worst time imaginable in a town whose population swells tenfold with sweaty tourists in July and August while the Florentines migrate to coastal towns like Viareggio and Carrara. I met my tinted and rouged housing agent, Lorenza Fiordelisi, at my apartment. A self-proclaimed Florentine *doc*—short for *di origine controllata*, meaning "of certified origin" and used to designate genuine Italian wine and food products—Lorenza waited in front of what she promised me was a quiet studio in a desirable part of town. The apartment was a few paces from the Ponte Vecchio, and the neighborhood hummed with pedestrian traffic, fancy stores, and advertisements announcing the city's temptations. The massive wooden doors and cobblestone courtyards of the neighborhood *palazzi*, "apartment buildings," seemed to hide—in the manner of gated American colleges—discreet wealth and rarefied interests. Lorenza introduced me to my landlord, a Florentine lawyer. He said hello and marched us inside without helping me with my bags. Upstairs, he presented me with a single-spaced document listing the studio's contents, from the cups and saucers to the heater and stove. He asked me to sign, but I told him I'd like to see what was actually in the apartment first. He and his wife harrumphed before insisting that I fork over the plump rental fee.

I went out for lunch after unpacking. The restaurants on my street, Borgo San Jacopo, posted one tourist menu after another in the commercial languages of the world, often accompanied by pictures. Fighting the crowds, I made it to the Ponte Vecchio and stared into the green-brown river. The streets surrounding the bridge brimmed with Internet cafés, sandwich shops, trinket stalls, and Coca-Cola vendors that catered to the white-sneaker crowd. I, too, had come to enjoy the city's artistic and cultural splendor, to collect my Tuscan recipes and Deruta ceramics while savoring the architecture of Alberti and the haughty ladies of Piero della Francesca. But something seemed off. I was used to the vigorous mercantilism of the Florentines and their polemical edge, distilled to compulsive perfection by my new landlord. After all, this was the city that invented modern banking, bankrolled the Renaissance, and created the first international currency-exchange mechanisms in the same piazzas where dollars, euros, and yuan are now traded. I understood that the Florentines are famously difficult to get to know—understandably so, given the level of tourism they've faced for centuries. But I also knew that once a Florentine accepts you as a friend, it is for life and in the spirit of boundless generosity. Still, on this gorgeous summer day the city looked spent. And its inhabitants kept me at the usual arm's length.

The changes I'd witnessed since 1987 were palpable. In the *centro storico*, the nameplates on the building façades listed a high percentage of foreign residents, especially Americans and Japanese, alongside the *i*-ending Tuscan names. At the finer restaurants I seldom heard the aspirated Tuscan accent— *"Hoha-Hola"* for "Coca-Cola"—and more often encountered singed blond tourists in tank tops asking for spaghetti and meatballs. I noticed the foreign shops selling bagels, chocolate chips, even the heretical *caffè americano*, which most Florentines consider to be more soup than coffee, especially in its decaffeinated version. Many Florentines could no longer afford to live in the *centro storico* and were exiled to either less picturesque parts of Chiantishire or the worn, industrial stepsister of Florence, Prato. The overwhelming level of tourism made for garbage-strewn streets, long museum lines, and little public space. So while *Saveur, Town & Country*, and the *Robb Report* continued to praise Florence's hidden trattorias, boutiques, and Renaissance treasures, its own citizens and disgruntled tourists of the two- and three-star set reviled the prices, crowds, and commercialism.

Later that night, hordes of tourists passed beneath the window of the supposedly *tranquillo* studio Lorenza had found for me, filling the air with shouts, laughter, and drunken declarations. And the Vespas roared. I phoned Lorenza around midnight to tell her that I was upset with her choice of location and landlord. She asked me why on earth I was calling at that hour and reminded me that the apartment overlooked an alley, so all this noise was impossible. The relentless pressure on the city's intimate scale—it was built *a misura umana*, "in human scale," locals and foreigners in the know like to say—made Florence feel more like a Euro Disney site than a real city. The tourism was nothing new. Young European nobles on their Grand Tour in the 1700s and 1800s would meet to study works of art only previously seen in books, just as today an international array of undergrads swaps cigarettes, Eurostar timetables, and directions to Florence's many Irish pubs.

A century or so after the Grand Tour, when Italy was no longer Goethe's "world's university" but its finishing school, Europeans traveled to Florence to give freer rein to passions that social protocols back home kept in check. In E. M. Forster's *A Room with a View*, Lucy Honeychurch and George Emerson fall in love after witnessing a murder over a trifle's worth of lire on a sunny day in the Piazza della Signoria. The shock of the event unleashes a flood of emotions in the two young people that their English upbringing can no longer repress. George submits ("Something tremendous has happened," he announces). Lucy will require many more pages, a broken engagement with the effete Cecil, and a dressing-down by George's freethinking father before she finally gets the "Italian" point.

I wanted to understand the city's legacy before it all went up in a blaze of Eurail passes, discount travel, and Gucci bags (real and fake). To everyone, even Katherine, I feigned an easy relationship with Florence, as if it were some prestigious college I had studied in years ago and kept going back to for summer reunions. In truth, Florence was like Italy itself to me: the embodiment of a high culture that I loved, but which always reminded me of its enormous distance from the world of my family. One doesn't travel to Cosenza's rivers, the Busento and Crati, to rinse the proverbial laundry, as Manzoni did in the Arno when he moved to Florence while translating *The Betrothed* into Tuscan. There's no Calabrian Santa Croce where they bury the illustrious southern Italian dead. My connection to the unforgiving Mezzogiorno was biological; my quest for Florence made me feel like Dante's beloved poet Arnaut Daniel—a man who hunted the hare with an ox, only to end up embracing the air.

After hanging up on Lorenza, I closed the green shutters over the alley and surrendered to my jet lag. But it was hours before sleep separated me from the sounds below, their din drowning out the currents of the Arno.

❋

Some five hundred years earlier, in the early winter of 1504, a group of artists and dignitaries gathered in Piazza della Signoria and stood before an arching marble statue, seventeen feet and six tons of fine Carrara marble chiseled by a young artist who had grown up just a few blocks away. The boy, Michelangelo Buonarroti, used to play with his friends in front of the nearby Basilica of Santa Croce. Now his *David* had drawn the leaders of his hometown to discuss where the colossus should go. The assembled included an elder statesman of Florentine art, Alessandro Filipepi (better known as Sandro Botticelli), and a rival of Michelangelo's from the Tuscan hills, an aloof artist with a perfect line and a scientific bent, named Leonardo da Vinci.

The scene suggests a fundamental element of Florentine history: its provincial quality. More than any cosmopolitan current, reigning fashion, or cult of personality, it has been Florence's families, guilds, schools, and grassroots organizations that have ushered in most of its epochal moments: the local poets who formed the *Dolce Stil Novo*, "Sweet New Style," and nurtured the young Dante's poetic sensibility; the workshops run by giants of Renaissance art, including Brunelleschi, architect of the city's Duomo, and Ghiberti, creator of the Gates of Paradise that grace the Baptistery; and the Neoplatonic academies of Florence's ruler, Lorenzo the Magnificent, who would discuss the mysteries of ancient philosophy with such humanists as Botticelli, Ficino, and Poliziano. But this neighborhood quality has a dark side. From the civil war that drove Dante into exile to the mercenary family politics that landed Renaissance Florence in French hands (and set in motion a profound cultural and economic decline), the city has chronically suffered from factional strife—the flip side of its communitarian spirit. According to the philosopher Benedetto Croce, all history is contemporary history, because we bother only with those past issues that still matter. All Florentine history, I would add, is *local* history, for everything there of global importance bears the imprint of a familiar piazza, a neighborhood café, or a conversation—if not a quarrel—among families, friends, or enemies.

For most, Florence's history ended about the time of Michelangelo's *David*: few believe that much of consequence occurred there after the Renaissance. In reality, few Italian cities have been as influential in shaping the modern life of their country, and at times even the world, as Florence. The city became the unofficial home of the Italian language in the 1700s and 1800s, when author-patriots including Vittorio Alfieri and Manzoni went to Florence to immerse themselves in the Tuscan dialect used by the *tre corone*, the "three crowns" of Italian literature: Dante, Petrarch, and Boccaccio. Florence also briefly served as the capital of the Italian nation in 1865, just four years after the unification, because the founders of Italy believed that the city's cultural heritage would have a cohesive political effect. In the early 1900s Florence became a principal site for Italian Futurism, an avant-garde movement that prized velocity, technological might, and creative violence—and rejected Italy's storied Renaissance heritage, claiming that it represented an unhealthy love of the past (*passatismo*). Many Italians still remember Florence for its heroic resistance to Fascism in World War II, when local partisans were among the first to free their city from Mussolini prior to the arrival of the Allied forces.

Closer to our own day, Florence's disastrous *alluvione*, the 1966 Flood of the Arno River, brought to the city the Angels of the Arno, young relief and rescue workers from all over the world, many of whom would participate in the international left-wing student movements. A witness to the relief effort, Senator Ted Kennedy noted its links with other youth protests already afoot in the 1960s. Arriving at the Biblioteca Nazionale near Santa Croce, Kennedy found a dark building, with no electricity and lighted with candles, set up for the rescue workers. Students, up to their waists in water, waded past him carrying precious manuscripts. Everywhere he looked in the great main reading room, hundreds of young people scurried to fulfill their tasks. "It was as if they knew that this flooding of the library was putting their soul at risk," he remarked.

Florence's Piazza Santa Croce during the 1966 Flood

The intervention of the Mud Angels was also less than divine. The Tuscan politician Vannino Chiti observed that though these young volunteers did indeed salvage the city's treasures, they also initiated the advent of mass tourism in Florence—which he called the city's "torment and delight," a prime source of income and employment that also poses a "permanent problem." In line with the progressive political traditions associated with the 1966 Flood, Florence of the early 2000s was the birthplace of the Laboratory for Democracy, an organization aimed at curbing perceived threats to political freedom by the Berlusconi government, particularly the use of the former premier's vast media empire for political ends. Local Florentine politics have once again become the center of national debate in recent years: The city's former mayor, Matteo Renzi, was appointed prime minister in 2014, after following President Barack Obama's example of becoming a celebrated author-politician while still in his thirties. Politically, his project of *rottamazione*, "overhaul," has become a buzzword for young Italians nationwide. His recent book, *Stil Novo*, evokes the poetic movement of Dante's youth and argues that politics and beauty must go hand in hand.

So why do so many overlook this rich modern history of Florence? And why has the city's legacy been reduced to the mass tourism I encountered that June evening along the Ponte Vecchio? David Leavitt wrote that Florence is a "delicate case" because it is home to so many Renaissance masterpieces that belong not just to the city, but to humanity. On that fateful day in 1504, local eminences, including Botticelli and Leonardo, could help decide where to put the *David*; today the whole world would have a say. I agree with Leavitt, but I don't think that he or any other writer fully explains why *modern* Florence is so often ignored while its illustrious past is idolized. Only after years of trying—and failing—to make Florence my own did I understand why it could be so difficult to hear, feel, and see its modern side.

Around the time of that 2005 trip, I visited Florence's Uffizi, the city's showpiece museum of Renaissance art. Its twin corridors usually brim with American tourists with backpacks, long-legged Scandinavians, bored Italian schoolchildren, and know-it-all aesthetes—all kinds of people except for an actual Florentine. But on this particular night, just as the museum was closing, I had the Botticelli Room and his painting the *Birth of Venus* almost all to myself. Staring at the canvas, I couldn't help but think of ancient times, when the human and divine could share sexual rapture. Despite her gorgeousness, Botticelli's Venus stimulated no erotic thoughts. She was beauty incarnate, too perfect to love but eternally poised for admiration. Eye level with the *Birth of Venus*, I realized that the ideas inspiring Botticelli—a sense of continuity between ancient and modern times, a cult of physical beauty, and a familiarity with mythology—had disappeared along with the Renaissance itself. I fell for Botticelli's Venus just as I realized how much distance separated me from the notion of beauty folded into her lily-white skin.

Albert Camus once wrote that in the Tuscan painter Piero della Francesca, "the spirit finds its meaning in the body," suggesting that the artist's earthy forms contain a love of life at odds with his own soul-searching age. Florence, for Camus and many other foreigners, cannot have a "modern" history, because it's locked in its own exquisite Renaissance past. Florence is hardly the only Italian city to

Botticelli's *The Birth of
Venus* in detail (1486)

be idealized in this way, but its case is especially instruc-
tive—or delicate, to use Leavitt's term—because of the international pull of its art.

Nowhere is our modern relation to Florence's heritage
more poignant than in Ugo Foscolo's poem "On Sepulchers" from 1807, written in response to a Napoleonic law
that banned burial within the city proper. Napoleon wanted
to abolish city graveyards for hygienic purposes, especially
to curtail the spread of infectious diseases from improperly
interred corpses, a rampant medical problem at that time
(and one that my gravedigger grandfather, Carmine Crocco,
would have well understood). But in Foscolo's view, for Italy
to come to life, the nation's living would have to remain
connected with its dead:

Florence, it was you who first
heard the song that cheered the exiled
Ghibelline [Dante], for all his anger. You
gave loving parents and your own [Tuscan] language
to the Muse's darling [Petrarch], the laureate poet
who wrapped the boy-god of love, naked
in Greece, naked in Rome, in the whitest
veil and returned him to the lap of Venus
in heaven. But your greatest bliss is this:
to have united in one temple the glory
of Italy—all that is left of its glory
since the undefended Alps and power's changing
fortunes have plundered our arms, wealth,
altars, fatherland, everything save memory.

Foscolo thought that Florence's art exuded a message of unity that could counter Italy's schisms. The tombs of Santa Croce and the Florentine cultural experience offered Italians the opportunity to recuperate a Renaissance humanism that Foscolo believed to be society's best hope for peace and progress.

One of Foscolo's contemporaries also felt Florentine art in the blood. In 1817 the French author Stendhal, a confirmed Italophile, visited the same Basilica of Santa Croce where Galileo, Machiavelli, Michelangelo, and others are interred. "I was ecstatic with the idea that I was in Florence, close to the masters whose tombs I had seen," Stendhal wrote. "Deep in the contemplation of sublime beauty, I reached the emotional point where we experience heavenly sensations. When I left Santa Croce, I had heart palpitations. The life flowed out of me and I was afraid I would fall."

Stendhal was not alone. The Florentine psychologist Graziella Magherini discovered a medical condition—which she later called "Stendhal's syndrome" in honor of its illustrious forebear—to describe the disorienting effect of Florentine art on many of its foreign visitors. "For many years," she said, "my attention was arrested by a peculiar phenomenon: the arrival in the emergency room of foreign tourists suddenly suffering from a psychic shock, some so strong that they asked to be taken to the psych ward." Magherini treated more than a hundred cases between 1988 and 1998, with symptoms ranging from fainting and suffocation to loss of identity. She noted that the slightest of details could set the illness in motion—even a splash of pigment from Botticelli. "Have you noticed the wind, the motion of the sea [in *The Birth of Venus*]? These details allow you to understand how many disturbing elements underlie this beautiful form."

Stendhal, for his part, was able to regain his composure only when he reached into his pocket and read from the book resting against his throbbing chest: Ugo Foscolo's poem "On Sepulchers."

A few days after my midnight call to Lorenza, she and I met for dinner in a trattoria called Pane e Olio, "Bread and Oil," one of the few affordable places in the *centro storico* where you could still hear the breathy accents of the city's workers. The spinach wilted in the display case, and there was no air conditioner inside the restaurant, only a single whirring fan against the savage heat. Lorenza, who lives on a meager pension and whatever housing commissions she can cull from

American colleges in Florence, loaded up on the salt-free bread.

I told her that I had to cut my visit short because of professional obligations back home.

"Non capisco, Gioè" ("I don't understand, Joe," which she pronounced "jo-AY," somehow making my name exotic), she said in shock. *"Veramente, non capisco."*

I made up something about a pressing work matter. Something that "couldn't wait." She nodded her head, but I knew she didn't buy my story. As in past years, I came to Florence alone that summer. I had left Katherine to return to my Italian fairyland. But from the moment I boarded the plane in North Carolina, I knew something was wrong. I was going to be gone for only six weeks, but I left Katherine just as our relationship was entering a new phase, one that would ask us to give up some of the things we loved in order to build a life together. Shortly before I left for Florence, Katherine had asked me to clarify the status of our relationship. She had no intention of living together "indefinitely," as she put it, if it wasn't heading somewhere. But I insisted on returning to Italy. Ostensibly, I was there to consult the usual archives and chase down Italian books. In truth, I had better access to research material in the efficient American university library system than in the hopeless Italian one. I came back to Florence because I was still pursuing that idea of high Italian culture—with its promise of a new-and-improved identity—that had first drawn me there in 1987.

That summer, I gave a lecture on Dante in a small Tuscan town where I had studied the poet years earlier. All through my talk I felt the same nausea I had suffered through on the morning of my flight from North Carolina, when I left Katherine to return to Florence. I was about to turn thirty-eight, unwed, childless. I was reading my paper on Dante, but I kept thinking, *Florence is no place to start building a life.* I couldn't change that I had been insulted freshman year by a pretty rich girl who questioned which Italy I belonged to. But I could do something about having come abroad and left behind the person I loved. *What is the point of a life that has never made a single sacrifice for love?* This was the lesson that Florence finally taught me. I never thought I would ask myself this question there.

Each night of my stay on Borgo San Jacopo I escaped the roar outside my window and called Katherine from an orange phone booth tucked in an alley by the Arno. As we spoke, the hot summer air by the river gave off its bittersweet fragrance, a mix of perfume, traffic exhaust, and olive oil. Florence could not change me into the European Italian I once dreamed of becoming. But other transformations had taken place. That first visit to Florence had triggered something that inspired me to become a professor of Italian. The art, the architecture, the food, the history, the haunches of Ammannati's Neptune—I would make a career of it.

After talking with Katherine on the last night of my trip, I stayed up well past midnight, reading to distract myself from the cries of the students and au pairs below my window. The book was E. M. Forster's *A Room with a View.* After Lucy and George fall in love in the shadows of murder and eventually marry, they return to the Pensione Bertolini, where they first met in Florence. Their sudden marriage has angered those closest to them: Lucy's mother, her ex-fiancé Cecil, and the parish priest Mr. Beebe. But Lucy and George are together now, and they look outside their window, as I looked past the green shutters and into the alley below, all of us gazing in the direction of the Arno. The book ends with Lucy and George finally together, their passion shared and their love requited. That summer, my relationship with Florence—at least the version of it that began when I was a student in 1987—finally ended, and I was relieved to let it go. Lucy and George, in the book's final phrase, feel the presence of a love more mysterious and greater than their own: "they heard the river, bearing down the snows of winter into the Mediterranean." I had never seen snow on the Arno, but I had seen my share of sun over the river and its empty early-morning streets. *What is the point of a life that has never made a single sacrifice for love?* There was nothing more I could ask of Florence.

Two weeks later, with a ring I had purchased on the Ponte Vecchio, I asked Katherine to marry me.

Epilogue: The Stones of Santa Croce

She said yes.

Our wedding took place on August 6, 2006, on a cloudless summer day in Bristol, Rhode Island, not far from the coastal town where I had grown up and my parents had raised their six children—and not far from the Little Italy I finally stopped running from. My mother and siblings were all there, and we feasted on brimming platters of antipasto, including a tray of my family's homemade soppressata. There were only a few representatives from the Old Country on hand: Giuseppina Fusaro, an ageless widow in her sixties who spoke the best English of all her Calabrian friends; Giovanni Crocco, whom another uncle of mine, Giancarlo Luzzi, had once tied up outside his Calabrian home so that my father could *acchiappa*, "grab," my mother to stage the ersatz rape that had risked jail and led to marriage. Uncle John, as we called him, was my mother's only living brother and had spent his first twenty years in Calabria, yet he would become as bona fide a New Jerseyite as Snooki and my tuxedoed Florentine classmate, Anthony. He smoked cigarettes and drank coffee all day long, and when I told him about the sites I'd visited in his home country, he would sneer, "Ah, Joey, why do you bother? You seen one statue, you seen 'em all."

There were no other siblings of my parents in attendance—and not a single member of the Council of Brothers that had tried to banish Maddalena for her infidelity in 1977 was on hand. My uncle Gianmaria on my father's side had died two months after my father, in 1995, his former tree trunk of a body ravaged by cancer. Many had been the times he would sit, head bowed, corpulent, alongside my father through a multicourse meal of pasta, meat, and stewed vegetables washed down with quarts of homemade red wine. They barely spoke during these savage repasts, their jaws grinding away in unbroken rhythm, like starving lions. Only Zio Francesco and Zio Giancarlo were alive that day I was married, but neither came (Bristol, a full hour's drive from Westerly, was considered a distant road trip). Cancer has since claimed Francesco; of all my father's siblings, only Giancarlo remains.

Dead too was Domenico Annunziato Bellacqua, alias Dom, defender of his adulterous wife and defier of his family honor code. Of that Council of Brothers, only one survives—the once fabulously potbellied Gianciotto, whose photos my father had blackened with Magic Marker during one of their many feuds, now slim, silver-haired, and approaching ninety. The same man whose jilted lover had once stabbed him in the chest and gone to jail as a result. He is the last Bellacqua dinosaur to roam the streets of Westerly's Little Italy, at the confluence of Pearl, Pierce, and Pond streets.

Nor were Cumara Amandina and her daughter Giuliana there. The connection between our families, the product of my father's chaste worship of my domestic-goddess god-mother, weakened after his death. Giuliana, the beautiful child who grew up to be an equally lovely woman, followed a path similar to mine: in most un-*fimminella* fashion, she had been living with a man in San Diego before I finally saw her again, shortly after Katherine died. We spent an afternoon walking through Wilcox Park in downtown Westerly. I was too grief-stricken to think of this as a "date," but her interest in my life and my daughter seemed more than cousinly. I looked into her blue eyes and remembered that star-crossed Easter rabbit all those years ago; now the bosom of my Calabrian childhood was opening up again, ready to smother me with protection as I dealt with my wife's death. We went for a coffee and, inevitably, the question of "how I was doing" came up.

"It was God's will," she said to me. "You have to believe that. It happened for a reason."

It wasn't fair of me to judge her for this. She could have just been trying to comfort me by saying something she didn't necessarily believe. Something to cushion the blow that I had been dealt. But whatever her intent, she had invoked the language of cause and effect. By then I had come to believe that there was no reason for what had happened. As Giuliana and I sipped our cappuccinos, I realized that she had not abandoned the faith of our people. Faced with my crisis, she reached out to the God who has comforted all the children of *la miseria*; I couldn't bring myself to this ancient Calabrian surrender.

For a long time after Katherine's death I couldn't visit Italy. It was too painful to go back to the place where, years earlier in Florence, I had discovered the depth of my love for her in a noisy apartment on Borgo San Jacopo. We shared some of our happiest times in Florence: shopping for pastry at Patrizio Cosi's under the arcades of Piazza Salvemini; strolling past the cenotaph of Dante in Piazza Santa Croce; wading into bowls of pesto at the Teatro del Sale, an eating club in the university district; sipping the espresso of Bar ChiaroScuro on the Corso; standing together beside Botticelli's lily-white allegories.

For three years I stayed away. Finally, in 2010, I returned to Florence to direct my college's study abroad program, twenty-three years after I myself had first arrived in Florence, an undergraduate in search of his Italian roots. I left our daughter, Isabel, behind with my family and visited the city alone. For the first few days I felt sick to my stomach. I missed Isabel, which was understandable enough, but I also longed for—to use that wooden term—*my former life.* Everywhere, the smells and sounds reminded me of Katherine. The first night, I went to the Teatro del Sale in hip Sant'Ambrogio. The first bite of *fusilli al ragù,* homemade pasta spindles in meat sauce, returned me to the Italian meals Katherine and I had shared. It's bad enough to wallow in or even dream about the past; I was feasting on it.

Halfway through my stay, the pain of these daily pleasures melted into less visceral, more atmospheric sensations. After a while the roasted, acrid taste of the espresso from ChiaroScuro didn't just remind me of Katherine. It filled my insides with chocolate warmth on the rainy, icy days. The roaring Vespas no longer only recalled the mornings I woke up beside her. They evoked my first student days in the 1980s in Piazza della Libertà, when I learned that ambient urban noise is as much a part of Italian life as compact cars and limoncello liqueur.

During my stay, I made plans to meet a friend at Villa I Tatti, former home of the art historian Bernard Berenson and now a center for Renaissance studies, affiliated with Harvard. It was a warm winter day, and we walked through gardens filled with sculptures and lemon trees, surrounded by the Tuscan hills. Everywhere I looked, smelled, touched was—there is no other word—*beauty*. I had learned all too well that beauty, like love, is not enough for this world: no amount of Tuscan light or Piero della Francesca could relieve the sorrow that had filled me since losing Katherine. But still, my surroundings struck me as an achievement worth acknowledging, even celebrating. After all, beauty was why I had chosen to spend so much of my life in Florence. And now I felt that this Florentine beauty—in Botticelli's *Venus*, in the bowls of ribollita, in the starlings flocking to Santa Maria Novella—just might help me heal. Had I been alone, I would have fallen to my knees by the orange trees of I Tatti.

When I returned from Florence a few days later, I gave Isabel a green raincoat with matching hat that I had purchased not far from the Duomo. The next day, I wrote to a friend describing what it had been like to go back to Italy for the first time after Katherine's death. The subject line read "My own two Italies." This time, however, I wasn't thinking of the Italy of the north and the south. I was thinking of the Italy of the living and the dead.

The Italy I found after Katherine died was filled with ghosts. Everywhere I turned, the streets and squares commemorated such and such a person or such and such an event. I passed museums that housed relics of the past, children who saw their grandparents every day, and family-owned restaurants that served decades-old recipes to decades-long clients. In the United States, death is something to avoid talking about and to treat as a disease that can be cured with the right diet and workout routine. In Italy, death is woven into the fabric of everyday life.

The commemoration and retrospection that went with Italian culture only intensified my feelings of loss. I kept returning, every year, to Santa Croce's tombs, hoping like a character out of a nineteenth-century novel—like Stendhal himself, Foscolo's copy of "On Sepulchers" pressed against his chest—that Italy would once again provide the freshness and delight, the silliness even, that I had once found in it. I visited the statue of Dante glaring over Santa Croce and looked into his eyes, as if trying to read the stars on the face of the sky. I also went back to Piazza Signoria and sought out the reassuring bulk and stern gaze of Ammannati's Neptune beneath the immobile clock hands of Palazzo Vecchio. But like all eyes made of stone, his just looked through me. I searched everywhere for the Italy I had lost—everywhere except for the one place and the one person that could restore it.

Shortly after Katherine died, I received an email from one of the paramedics who had responded to her accident. My wife's crash had occurred while I was proctoring an exam at Bard. She was driving to SUNY New Paltz, where she had enrolled as a B.A. student in history, returning to college after deciding to end her career as an actor in New York. I have forgotten the words of the paramedic's note, only that she wanted to express her sorrow over what had happened and to see how my daughter was doing. I stared dumbfounded at the message. My gratitude for this anonymous woman, who had helped save my daughter's life, was so profound that it paralyzed me. I could not answer.

Not even the wonder of my daughter's birth could penetrate the grief that descended on me. I had the support of my family, friends, an entire academic community. But it wasn't enough. After a lifetime of pushing forward at all costs, counting the paces I put between myself and Little Italy, I circled backward. Back to my family, their unconditional care, and our people's *miseria*. The move was natural: Calabria had made my family experts in death.

In a noncredit introductory course on Southern Italian Child Rearing, my mother taught me how to deal with an infant's fussy appetites, irregular sleep patterns, violent mood swings, and sudden spurts of growth. While my friends read books about tiger parenting or super baby food, Isabel's *nonna* relied entirely on intuition. She had two traits that eluded my cohort of highly educated parents: calm and, when necessary, indifference. From vomiting to fevers, nothing Isabel did fazed her. Plugged in to the rhythms of my daughter's life just as her birth mother would have been, my mother poured centuries of Calabrian nurturing into Isabel's developing consciousness. Isabel was entering life with the same ideas and practices that had produced my parents and their fatalistic worldview. Meanwhile, her father plugged away in the land of Dante and Michelangelo.

In the spring of 2012, I traveled from Rome's American Academy to Villa La Pietra, a fifty-seven-acre enclave of gardens, olive groves, stucco houses, and Renaissance art on the outskirts of Florence. The former home of the art collector Harold Acton, the property now houses the NYU Florence program, which had invited me there to lecture. I planned to speak about what happens to a city when it risks becoming a living museum that focuses more on preserving its past glories than on creating new ones. The title of my paper was "Florence After Florence: Modern Afterlife of a Renaissance City."

Acton's house stood on a hill encircled by other slopes of land, an undulating green wave punctuated by the slender elegance of cypresses. A short cab ride from the center of town, the main entrance to Villa La Pietra lies hidden on a nondescript street removed from the city's cultural attractions. Inside the gate, the property burst open like a bud. My cab negotiated the long, dramatically pitched driveway that led from the entrance to the main villa, and I was given the keys to a room on the upper floor. Once upstairs, I threw open the wooden shutters to a panorama of hillside villages spread out over a green Tuscan carpet. Finally, after a quarter century of visiting Florence, I had my room with a view.

Later that day, after a private tour of Acton's home and collection, I went to the podium and began my talk with lines from Dante's *Paradiso*:

> *Se mai continga che 'l poema sacro*
> *al quale ha posto mano e cielo e terra,*
> *sì che m'ha fatto per molti anni macro,*
> *vinca la crudeltà che fuor mi serra*
> *del bello ovile ov' io dormi' agnello,*
> *nimico ai lupi che li danno guerra;*

> *con altra voce omai, con altro vello*
> *ritornerò poeta, e in sul fonte*
> *del mio battesmo prenderò 'l cappello.*

> (Should it ever come to pass that this sacred
>   poem [*The Divine Comedy*],
> to which both Heaven and earth have set their hand
> so that it has made me lean for many years,
>   should overcome the cruelty that locks me out
> of the fair sheepfold where I slept as a lamb,
> foe of the wolves at war on it,
>   with another voice then, with another fleece,
> shall I return a poet and, at the font,
> where I was baptized, take the laurel crown.)

The audience included students and academics as well as an actual Angel of the Arno, one of the relief workers who had helped rescue the city's art during the 1966 Flood. I described to them how Dante's words revealed his nostalgia for Florence, an example of the city's pull on exiles who, long after they lost their *Firenze*, created an imaginary version of it that had little to do with the real one. As with all such places, this absent homeland was unattainable. I was speaking, ostensibly, about Dante; I was speaking, actually, about myself.

Before my talk, I spent the morning in downtown Florence, where I planned to take Isabel on a tour of Santa Croce, the basilica guarded by the fierce statue of Dante and home to Italy's most hallowed burial ground—as well as the site that incited such reverie in Stendhal that he suffered palpitations. I had no need of a guidebook. Foscolo's "On Sepulchers," which celebrated Santa Croce as the home of an eternal Italian spirit, had inspired me to write a scholarly book that explored how the cultural traditions embodied by this basilica helped fuel Italian unification and create the modern myth of Italy.

As a kid, I had learned the myths of America—George Washington and his cherry tree, Paul Revere and his midnight ride—stories that helped connect me to my parents' adopted country. Patriotism worked its magic: my blood was pure Italian via Calabria, but through these tales I developed a connection to a new land. Later, the books I would read and study, especially Dante, nourished my growing love of Italy. But it was only "On Sepulchers" that had made Italy my second home. The poem gave me the one thing that Italian American culture, with its folk songs, homespun recipes, sepia photographs, and artery-busting sauces could not: a foundation myth. "On Sepulchers" closes with a description of Homer burrowing into the burial vaults of Troy to sing to future generations about Italy's rebirth. Foscolo offered a narrative about the origins of an Italy that belonged to citizens and immigrants alike, for it showed how Italy's roots dug deeper than the north-south divide, the language question, recipes for blood pudding, and exporting of *la miseria*. I was not a true child of Calabria as my parents were. But we were all in some way the children of Foscolo's Trojans.

Isabel was impressed by none of this. All that mattered to her was finding the next gelato, and she was lucky that just a few blocks from Santa Croce stood Vivoli, the city's oldest and most acclaimed gelateria, which once made its gelato from snow in the nearby mountains. As usual, she wrangled to get the largest size permissible. I prayed that all the *cioccolato fondente* wasn't stunting her growth.

Her face smeared in the zebra stripes of *stracciatella*, Isabel gamely entered Santa Croce. Finally, after years of traveling to Italy without her while she stayed behind in Rhode Island with my family, I was back on my feet and finding a balance between raising her and pursuing my career. She was old enough to parrot the Italian words I tried to teach her, from the simple *ciao* and *buon appetito a tutti* to the phonetic adventures of Trastevere and Palatino. Walking with her beside me in the Circus Maximus or scaling the steps together along the Janiculum, my body trembled with a joy I had never felt before, so powerful was the sense of relief—of *survival*—that we had made it through the long years since Katherine's death, and now we were finally in Italy together. I could tell her none of this. I couldn't even form these words to myself as her pink mini–Chuck Taylors smacked against the cobblestones. I had been obsessed, as a scholar, with afterlives—how Dante has been read from one generation to the next, how a Renaissance city such as Florence faces the modern world. With Isabel in Italy, I was facing a private afterlife: the Italy I had long known was gone forever, replaced by the one I was seeing now for the first time through my daughter's four-year-old eyes.

I started our tour of Santa Croce, as always, at Foscolo's statue. The inside of the church was as spare as the hollowed belly of a ship turned upside down. As I thought about the famous dead housed in the womb of the church, my eyes looked through the heights and into the wooden ceiling. I was back in Florence among the spirits I had spent my life studying, and I was here with the daughter who somehow, miraculously, had made it to the side of the living just before her mother expired.

I can't remember what I said to Isabel inside Santa Croce, only that the visit closed a circle that began in 1946, when my father pretended to rape my mother so he could marry her. I had to study Italy to understand my family's history, because only by grasping the complexity of writers such as Dante could I get the full picture of the culture that had made—and in my father's case, unmade—them. Outside, in Piazza Santa Croce, the usual bands of tourists milled from one leather shop to the next. Above, the cloudless blue sky poured down warm sunshine, the first good light after a series of rainy days. Somehow, a peasant marriage forged in a criminal act had culminated, more than sixty years later, in an afternoon idyll among artisanal gelato and Renaissance statuary. Italy and Italian America would always be separated by history and fact, but here—in a story that connected elements as different as my father's immigrant journey and Alessandro Manzoni's quest for a national language—they coalesced.

Isabel would never know her grandfather, the man who, like Aeneas, had ferried his family from an ancient land to a new one, unsure of what lay in store but certain about the degree of sacrifice that the journey would entail. I watched my daughter on the cobblestones and felt that my own voyage to Italy had come full circle, culminating in a new generation that could not feel the split between my father's Calabria and Dante's Florence as intensely as I had. Free from the reservoirs of *la miseria* I inherited from my parents, my daughter would likely stare one day at black-and-white photographs of a lost Calabrian world and wonder how on earth she was related to it. She would feel something denied to me as the child of immigrants: nostalgia, and with this longing become something alien to me in my ethnic limbo—a hyphenated "Italian-American."

All around us, the sunburned tourists moved through Santa Croce, pilgrims like me when I first arrived in Florence. Life had given me a second chance. My daughter was playing among the statues, in what Foscolo called the *tempio dell'itale glorie*, "temple of Italian glory." There were no monuments to the generations of Calabrians who had toiled for centuries before my parents fled Acri for America, no markers for the Carmine Croccos and Domenico Bellacquas that shared Isabel's and my southern Italian blood. I had spent my working life teaching and studying Italy, chasing a dream of it that reconciled the brutal world of my family and millions of immigrants like them with the cultural splendors I made into a career. But none of this, no majesty of Michelangelo's line or wondrous gaze of Galileo at the heavens, could make my Italy whole again—nothing could, except the love that streamed like starlight from my rescued daughter, an explosion of life amid the stone and marble.

Notes

The Calabrian proverb from the epigraph, submitted by Tom Lucente, is drawn from www.circolocalabrese.org/culture/calabria-proverbs.asp (accessed on April 19, 2013). References to Dante's *Divine Comedy* are to the translation and edition by Jean and Robert Hollander (New York: Anchor, 2000–2007). Translations are my own unless otherwise indicated. References to Giuseppe Tomasi di Lampedusa's novel and Percy Bysshe Shelley's letters are to, respectively, *The Leopard*, trans. Archibald Colquhoun (New York: Pantheon, 2007); and *The Letters of Percy Bysshe Shelley*, ed. Roger Ingpen, 2 vols. (London: Pitman, 1912).

INTRODUCTION: THE WITCH OF NAPLES
Works cited include Bill Emmott, *Good Italy, Bad Italy: Why Italy Must Conquer Its Demons to Face the Future* (New Haven: Yale University Press, 2012); and Virgil, *The Aeneid*, trans. Robert Fagles (New York: Penguin, 2008).

1. CARNAL VIOLENCE
The biographical information and details regarding my parents' marriage come from a series of recorded interviews with my mother, Yolanda Luzzi, in July 2005. For the *Times* article on *Jersey Shore* in Florence by Gaia Pianigiani and Rachel Donadio, "Like Seaside Heights, but with a Duomo," see: www.nytimes.com/2011/07/31/arts/television/jersey-shore-goes-to-florence-italy.html?pagewanted=all

&_r=0 (accessed on January 8, 2013). For excerpts from Camille Paglia's lecture on *The Sopranos*, see the online version of *The Pennsylvania Gazette* (January–February 2002): www.upenn.edu/gazette/0102/0102gaz3 .html (accessed on August 21, 2012). The episode from HBO's *The Sopranos* discussed is "Commendatori" (season 2, no. 4), written, produced, and directed by David Chase.

2. BLOOD PUDDING

I interviewed Petrini at New York's Italian Cultural Institute in May 2012. Works cited include Dante, *De vulgari eloquentia*, trans. Steven Botterill (Cambridge, U.K.: Cambridge University Press, 1996); Carlo Petrini, *Slow Food: The Case for Taste*, trans. William McCuaig (New York: Columbia University Press, 2003), and *Slow Food Nation: Why Our Food Should Be Good, Clean, and Fair*, trans. Clara Furlan and Jonathan Hunt (New York: Rizzoli, 2007); and Gary Shteyngart, *Super Sad True Love Story* (New York: Random House, 2010). Bill Buford's *Heat* (New York: Knopf, 2006) and John Varriano's *Tastes and Temptations: Food and Art in Renaissance Italy* (Berkeley: University of California Press, 2009) discuss the colors, respectively, of Florentine and Venetian cooking.

3. A FAMILY AFFAIR

Works cited include Edward C. Banfield, *The Moral Basis of a Backward Society* (Glencoe, IL: Free Press, 1958); Malcom Gladwell, *Outliers* (New York: Little, Brown, 2008); Joseph LaPalombara, "Italy: Fragmentation, Isolation, Alienation," in *Political Culture and Political Development*, eds. Lucian W. Pye and Sidney Verba (Princeton: Princeton University Press, 1965); Alessandro Manzoni, *The Betrothed*, trans. Bruce Penman (London: Penguin, 1972); Giuseppe Mazzini, *The Duties of Man and Other Essays*, ed. Thomas Jones (London: Dent, 1915); and Robert D. Putnam, with Robert Leonardi and Raffaella Y. Nanetti, *Making Democracy Work: Civic Traditions in Modern Italy* (Princeton: Princeton University Press, 1993). For discussions of the *bamboccioni*, see *Der Spiegel* (October 8, 2007): www.spiegel.de/international/europe/tax-breaks-for -big-babies-italy-lures-mamma-s-boys-away-from-home-a-510004 .html (accessed on August 24, 2012); Malcolm Moore, *Daily Telegraph* (October 5, 2007): www.telegraph.co.uk/news/worldnews/1565237

/Italys-mammas-boys-given-cash-to-fly-nest.html (accessed on August 24, 2012); and Nick Squires, *Telegraph* (September 21, 2011): www.telegraph.co.uk/news/worldnews/europe/italy/8777301/Italian-parents-bring-in-lawyers-to-evict-41-year-old-stay-at-home-son.html (accessed on August 24, 2012).

4. THE FIG TREE AND THE IMPALA

The literary critic I refer to on p. 106 is Georg Lukács, *The Historical Novel*, trans. Hannah and Stanley Mitchell (Lincoln: University of Nebraska Press, 1970). For information on the Italian language from unification to the present, see Tullio De Mauro, *Storia linguistica dell'Italia unita* (Bari: Laterza, 1963); Christopher Duggan, *The Force of Destiny: A History of Italy Since 1796* (Boston: Houghton Mifflin, 2008); and Giulio Lepschy, *Mother Tongues and Other Reflections on the Italian Language* (Toronto: University of Toronto Press, 2002). References to Vico and Horace are, respectively, to *The New Science of Giambattista Vico*, trans. Thomas Bergin and Max Fisch (Ithaca: Cornell University Press, 1984); and *Horace: Satires, Epistles, and Ars poetica*, trans. H. Rushton Fairclough (Cambridge: Harvard University Press, 1929).

5. NO SOCIETY

John Hopper discusses Venice's grim prospects in "Population Decline Set to Turn Venice into Italy's Disneyland," *The Guardian* (August 25, 2006): www.theguardian.com/world/2006/aug/26/italy.travelnews (accessed on January 15, 2013). For selections from the panel "Italy Today: Politics, Society, the Economy," see www.aarome.org/events/ongoing (accessed on August 22, 2012). For Leopardi's essay, see *Discorso sopra lo stato presente dei customi degl'italiani*, ed. Marco Dondero (Milan: Rizzoli, 1998). The original Italian quotation from *The Leopard* is from *Il Gattopardo* (Rome: Feltrinelli, 1980). See also Castiglione, *The Book of the Courtier*, trans. George Bull (London: Penguin, 2004). Beppe Severgnini's article appeared in the *Financial Times* on January 18, 2012. For my reading of Shelley's letter, see chapter 2 of *Romantic Europe and the Ghost of Italy* (New Haven: Yale University Press, 2008); the article originally appeared as "Italy Without Italians: Literary Origins of a Romantic Myth," *Modern Language Notes: Italian Issue* 117 (2002): 48–83. For the quote from Berlusconi on p. 154, see Paul Ginsborg, *Silvio Berlusconi: Television, Power and Patrimony* (London: Verso, 2004). I interviewed Prodi at his office in Bologna in April 2012. For Prodi's view that Italians have "tactics" but no "final goal," see "Profile: Romano Prodi," by David Willey, *BBC News*, news.bbc.uk/2/hi/europe/299254.stm (accessed on October 28, 2013).

6. FLORENCE AFTER FLORENCE

For a description of the unveiling of Michelangelo's *David*, see R. W. B. Lewis, *The City of Florence: Historical Vistas and Personal Sightings* (New York: Farrar, Straus and Giroux, 1994). See also Albert Camus, *Noces* (Paris: Gallimard, 1950); E. M. Forster, *A Room with a View* (London: Penguin, 1992); David Leavitt, *Florence: A Delicate Case* (New York: Bloomsbury, 2002); Graziella Magherini's interview with Maria Barnas, *Metropolis M* 4 (2008), http://metropolism.com/magazine/2008-no4/confrontaties/english (accessed on April 21, 2013); and Stendhal, *The Private Diaries of Stendhal*, trans. Robert Sage (New York: Doubleday, 1954). The quotations from Ted Kennedy and Vannino Chiti are taken from, respectively, www.catpress.com/allu/eng/intvents.htm and www.catpress.com/allu/eng/intventi.htm (accessed on March 19, 2006). For translations of Ugo Foscolo's "On Sepulchers," see Peter Burian's "Ugo Foscolo: *Sepulchers*," *Literary Imagination* 4 (2002): 17–30.

Acknowledgments

This book has benefited from the wisdom of my *primi lettori*, the "first readers" who generously combed through multiple drafts and offered invaluable suggestions for improvement: Helena Baillie, Rebecca Godfrey, Ross Guberman, Joy Harris, and Scott McGill. My sister Rose Luzzi Durham gave precious assistance in finding the family documents and photographs that fired my imagination at all stages of writing, and Jacopo Gorini's skill and *sprezzatura* helped me negotiate some tricky linguistic issues.

I have been blessed to work with the talented and supportive team at FSG, especially Miranda Popkey and Stephen Weil, who walked me through the many aspects of this book's production with great care.

I owe a special debt of gratitude to my editor and friend, Jonathan Galassi. Without his literary insights and his belief in this project, *My Two Italies*—and the connection it has given me to my family's lost Italian world—would not exist.

Grazie di cuore a voi tutti.

ILLUSTRATION CREDITS